GROUNDED

— upon —

God's Word

GROUNDED

— upon —
God's Word

The Life and Labors of Jakob Ammann

Andrew V. Ste. Marie
Mike Atnip

SERMON ON THE MOUNT
PUBLISHING

Manchester, MI

ISBN 978-1-68001-030-5

Library of Congress Control Number: 2020949194

For additional titles and other material by the same authors, contact:

Sermon on the Mount Publishing

P.O. Box 246

Manchester, MI 48158

(734) 428-0488

the-witness@sbcglobal.net

www.kingdomreading.com

Our Mission

To obey the commands of Christ and to teach men to do so.

About the Cover

The front cover portrays Jakob Ammann in a 17th-century Swiss home, reading the Bible. The back cover portrays his wife and daughter at a spinning wheel. The clothing of the Ammann family is based on artistic portrayals of early 19th-century Swiss and French Anabaptist dress.

Cover art by Peter Balholm.

First printing—December 2020—5,913 copies

Second printing—POD edition

Third printing—June 2023—5,000 copies

Dedication

This series is dedicated to the Lord Jesus Christ,

the King of Saints.

This volume is also dedicated to Chester Weaver, whose enthusiastic encouragement and wise counsel has added much to my life—particularly my pursuit of historical studies.
Thank you, brother!
~A.V.S.

Acknowledgments

Work on this book began in 2012. In the eight years of writing, the authors have accumulated debts of gratitude to many people.

First, we thank the Lord Jesus Christ, in Whom we live and move and have our being, Who motivates our work, life, and worship. May He be honored through this book.

We thank Edsel Burdge, Joseph Stoll, Aaron Stoll, Dale Burkholder, Chester Weaver, Matthew Brubacher, Ed Kline, and Leroy Beachy for reading the manuscript and offering helpful critiques and encouragement. Extra-special thanks to Dr. Hanspeter Jecker, whose decades of research in Swiss archives made his input extremely valuable and who saved us from several embarrassing mistakes (and who contributed an illustration as well). Thanks to Vincent and Barbara Ste. Marie and the rest of the Ste. Marie family for their unceasing support, encouragement, and input.

Peter Balholm did a stunning piece of art for the cover, and Justin Ebersole completed the job with a fantastic cover design. Clement Ebersole helped with the interior design. Jennifer Burdge copyedited the text. Thomas Kaltenreider has investigated the Ammann family home in Erlenbach and contributed photographs of the building which he feels is the right one. Dean Taylor and David Bercot also contributed photographs. Robert Baecher contributed scans of Ammann's signatures. Thanks also to Jennifer Burdge and Ashley Niro for copyediting.

Thanks to the scholars whose work has been the foundation of this book—especially John D. Roth, Hanspeter Jecker, and Robert Baecher. Without their diligent work in piecing together the puzzle pieces of Ammann's life, we would have nothing to say. Thanks also to the Mennonite Historical Society for allowing us to use their translations of primary sources, and to Josiah Beachy, John B. Martin, and Isaac Lowry for their translation work.

Finally, thanks to you, our readers—readers of our past books, this book, and (hopefully) future books. Without readers, we would have no reason to write. Thank you!

Cross Bearers

Series

The ***Cross Bearers Series*** is presented to acquaint readers with men and women who followed in Jesus' steps. Today's reader is inundated with biographies of those who professed Christ, but who did not teach and practice what Jesus taught and practiced.

One of Jesus' plainest teachings is that "whosoever doth not bear his cross, and come after me, cannot be my disciple" (Luke 14:27). Yet how often we are told that Jesus died on the cross for us so that we do not need to die! Peter tells us in I Peter 2:21, "For even hereunto were ye called: because Christ also suffered for us, leaving us an example, that ye should follow his steps."

Our "heroes" help define who we are and who we intend to be. Today's youth are in desperate need of role models who go beyond saying, "Lord, Lord!" While Jesus is the Ultimate Example, we can also learn from those who strove to imitate Him. We can learn from their mistakes, as well as from their glorious victory over self, sin, Satan, and the world through the power of the Spirit that worked in them.

The stories presented in the *Cross Bearers Series* will be drawn from various ages and churches. While "historical fiction" may be easier to read, these biographies will present the stories using a minimum of author imagination. However, the stories will be salted and peppered with other content (artwork, photos, and text sidebars) to capture the context of the culture in which they walked.

The ultimate goal of the *Cross Bearers Series* is to provoke all of us to follow these men and women as they followed Christ.

TABLE OF CONTENTS

Timeline

1618	Thirty Years' War begins
1644	Jakob Ammann born
1648	Thirty Years' War ends
1653	Swiss Peasants' War
1655	Ammann family moves to Oberhofen
1660s	Jakob Ammann marries Verena Stüdler
1662	Ulrich Ammann born
1670-1690	Outbreak of Anabaptism in Bernese Oberland
c. 1678-79	Jakob Ammann joins the Anabaptists
1680	Jakob Ammann probably leaves Bern
1683	First permanent Mennonite settlement in North America (Germantown, Pennsylvania)
1690	Ammann preaching by this time
c. 1690	Jakob's father Michel begins associating with Anabaptists, eventually joins them
1693-94	Emmental/Oberlander (Reistian-Amish) controversy and division
Summer 1694	Ammann arrested, escapes
1694-95	Many Oberland Anabaptists migrate to Alsace; Jakob Ammann serves as elder/bishop there
1695	Michel Ammann dies
1694-1700	Numerous attempts for reconciliation between Reistians and Amish
1711	Ulrich Ammann tries again to make peace with the Reistians
1711	Anabaptist exodus from Bern
1712	Anabaptists expelled from Alsace
Before 1730	Death of Jakob Ammann
After 1733	Death of Ulrich Ammann

CHAPTER 1

Wartime Babies

et your mind wander back to the 1640s. Perhaps you excelled in history class at school and can remember some exciting historical event from that decade. What do you remember about the 1640s?

If you remember anything, you likely remember wars in 17th-century Europe—religious wars! On the continent, the Thirty Years' War is ending. Of course, nobody really knew that the long series of wars between the Catholics and the Protestants[1] were finally concluding; we only know that fact by looking back at the events. Europe is tired of war, or at least should be. Portions of Germany have lost the majority of their inhabitants, with half of the males now dead. The average drop in population for the German states is 25-40%.

In England, a middle-aged man is going through a bout of depression and finally has a religious experience. He becomes stoutly Puritan and sees England as "full of sin" and in serious need

---

1   The wars were not exactly drawn along Catholic/Protestant lines, nor were they entirely religious in character. However, religion was one of the major underlying sources of contention in the early stages of the conflict.

of spiritual reform: All residues of Roman Catholicism must be purged! Oliver Cromwell will eventually rise to the highest levels of politics, dragging his bloody sword through the land right alongside his Bible. He is one of the 59 men to sign his name to the death sentence of King Charles I—using the latter part of Numbers 35:33 as a rationale.[2] But after he dies and Charles II takes the throne, Cromwell's body is dug up—on the twelfth anniversary of Charles I's execution—and posthumously executed. The severed head is displayed outside of Westminster Abbey for the next 24 years. Oliver Cromwell's name is enshrined in England to this day, right beside words like "hero" and "liberator"—as well as "genocide" and "dictator."

But now we lift our eyes beyond the clang of sword and boom of gun to the quiet, upper[3] valleys of the Swiss Canton of Bern. It is Monday, February 12, 1644. We can imagine a young married couple emerging from their home above the village of Erlenbach im Simmental[4] with something—someone!—bundled tightly in a blanket. Two children toddle excitedly in their parents' footsteps through the creaky-cold snow as they make the descent toward the village chapel, about half a mile below their large chalet.

The bundle contains their newest joy, whom they have named Jakob. By Canton law, they must baptize their new child within fourteen days of birth. Had they lived in the city, the same law specified eight days. Did they carry little Jakob to the Erlenbach chapel out of duty and fear of Canton law, or out of love for his

---

2   ". . .the land cannot be cleansed of the blood that is shed therein, but by the blood of him that shed it."

3   Upper, in this case, means south of the city of Bern. The Aar River begins high in the Alps and flows north.

4   The name is rather long, but we need to use the full name since there are several Erlenbachs in Switzerland. The "im Simmental" is German for "in the Simme Valley." Simmental cattle got their name from the valley.

The Erlenbach Reformed chapel, where little Jakob Ammann was baptized as a baby in February 1644.

soul? After all, if Jakob is not baptized, he cannot inherit property. Baptism and citizenship are closely interwoven in 17th-century Switzerland—in fact, inseparable. There are fines for disobeying the baptism law.

Or were Michel and Anna Ammann concerned for the spiritual benefits of baptism? According to the prevalent teaching of their day, little Jakob had inherited the guilt of Adam's sin and needed to be "washed" from that guilt. To not baptize the child would be risking an eternity in hell if he died!

We will likely never know the parents' motives, but we do know with certainty that on February 12, 1644, Jakob Ammann[5] was

---

5   Other spellings encountered in the sources include Jacob Ammen, Jacob Amen, Jacques Aman, Jacob Aman, Jacqui Aman, Jacquy Aman, Jacquy Amand, Yacob Amen, Yacob Ami, Jacqui Amand, Jacob Ami, Jaggi Amman, and Yägi Amen. He usually signed his name "iA" and sometimes "i.AMME." In this book we will consistently use the spelling seen here, except in quotes.

baptized in the Erlenbach Reformed Church.[6] The chapel still stands, the *Taufrodel* (Baptismal Record) still exists, and little "Yaggi"[7]—the innocent little recipient of infant baptism that day—still exerts a positive influence on tens of thousands, over three and a half centuries later. Hundreds of thousands have been, and still are being, affected by his decisions. He, like Oliver Cromwell, had a vision for a purified church. But unlike Oliver, Jakob never tried to cleanse the church by political means and a bloody sword.

And yet, little Yaggi would gain a reputation as a troublemaker, a tyrant, a dictator, one who swiftly excommunicated those who hesitated to agree with him.

Jakob Ammann made some serious mistakes in his life. Who has not? But worse than that, those who opposed him wrote most of the history books for many generations. Jakob's mistakes were held in the forefront again and again, until the mention of his name could only conjure negative stereotypes.

We will look at his life outside of the stereotypes. After all, Jakob acknowledged his mistakes. He confessed and apologized. He even placed himself in the *Bann*,[8] asking his antagonists to receive him back.

The following chapters are the story of Jakob Ammann, de-stereotyped. However, we must first look at the historical forces that shaped Jakob and his contemporaries.

---

6   The date of his birth is unknown, but was most likely within two weeks preceding his baptism.

7   German "J" sounds like our English "Y." Thus Jacob sounds like Yacob. The Swiss habitually added an "i" (li) to many names as an endearing diminutive. Thus Jacob became Yaggi, equivalent to our Jakie. Jacob Ammann is referred to as Yaggi in some historical documents.

8   The German spelling of a word that means, in its root sense, the same as our English word "ban" and refers to excommunication. We will meet this concept later in the story.

CHAPTER 2

Plague, War, and the Little Ice Age

We cannot comprehend Jakob Ammann entirely unless we place him in the greater context of European history. Can we understand 17th-century Europeans, for example, without considering the plague?

We modern North Americans have no idea whatsoever what life would look like if, on a routine basis, about 1/3 of our neighbors would suddenly die within a few days. Not just once, but every so many years, on an unpredictable basis, the plague raged through Europe. Some small villages were entirely depopulated, although most of them had some survivors. In 1612, the Canton of Zürich lost 1/3 of its population to the tiny bacteria that traveled in the fleas that hitchhiked on the backs of the common rat.

No one had any idea, though, at that time, who or what was responsible for the Black Death. When the plague would strike a town, many would flee. The more kind-hearted ones would help to bury the dead, sometimes paying the death penalty for their charity.

A small percentage who contracted the plague would survive. But the *fear*! Fear that we can only imagine today, sitting in our

COVID-19 and the Plague

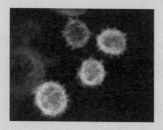 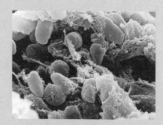

As this book neared completion, the COVID-19 pandemic rocked the world. With the great fear of infection which swept the world, people today can now relate to medieval Europeans' fear of the plague. However, COVID-19 is nowhere near as dangerous as the plague. Whereas the death rate of COVID-19 is less than 1%, the death rate of the plague was 30-100% (if left untreated—and the medieval Europeans had no antibiotics with which to treat patients).

armchairs reading statistics like 1/3 of the population of Europe dying from the plague.

Then There was War

For Europe, the 1600s were all about war. One has to search very carefully to find a year in the seventeenth century in which no European kingdom was warring against another. In fact, some historians consider the seventeenth century to be one of history's most combative eras.[1] First it was the Poles and Swedes (1600-1629), then the English and the French (1627-1629), wars between "The Three Kingdoms" (British, Irish, and Scots) from 1639-1653,

---

1   Not just in Europe, but in Asia as well, with the Qing dynasty overtaking the Ming dynasty in China, with an estimated 25 million casualties.

From 1618 to 1648, the Thirty Years' War devastated Europe, even as numerous smaller conflicts were being fought at the same time.

the rebellion of the Portuguese against Spanish oversight (1640-1668), the Thirteen Years' War between the Poles and Russians (1654-1667), then the Swedes and Poles again from 1655-1660, then the French and the Dutch (1672-1678), and finally the Nine Years' War (1688-1697) between France and many of the other European nations. There were also numerous other minor conflicts and several wars with the Ottoman Turks.

And the "Big One"

The previous paragraph left out the war that affected Europe the most: The Thirty Years' War that stretched from 1618-1648. Just as modern North Americans have no idea what it was like to deal with the Black Plague that killed 1/3 of Europe, we have no idea what it was like to suffer from three decades of war that wiped away almost half the population. For thirty years, armies marched across Europe, doing what armies do, both to soldiers and civilians. The Thirty Years' War was one of the most destructive armed conflicts

Europe ever experienced. Although "only" eight million people are estimated to have died—compared to World War II's 15-20 million[2]—the total percentage of population loss is quite distinct: About 40% of the European population died in the Thirty Years' War, compared to about 10% in World War II.[3] In some places in what is now Germany, the loss was about 75% of the population. On average, half the males in Europe died because of the Thirty Years' War: some because of fighting, others because of starvation or disease spread by the marauding armies.

Jakob Ammann was born near the end of this conflict, and without a doubt it affected his way of life. Although Switzerland was spared from any direct conflict on its soils, many Swiss mercenaries were hired by various other kingdoms. This boosted the Swiss economy, since the money brought home by the mercenaries added to the local economy, and prices for agricultural commodities were up because of the conflict.

But the Thirty Years' War touched Jakob even more directly. By the time the last army had trampled through Alsace and the Palatinate to the north, practically every vestige of civilization had been wiped away. If the inhabitants had not been killed, they had fled to the nooks and crannies in the woods. Buildings were burned and fields were growing up in brush. It has been said that one could walk for 20-30 miles and not see another human soul.

The lords of those lands were quite eager to find some settlers to make the lands productive once again, and Swiss Anabaptists were being forced into exile. That match was perfect. The hardworking, honest Anabaptists were even given a bit more freedom of religion, although open evangelism was still forbidden. The owners of the

---

2   In Europe. The worldwide figure for World War II is about 75 million.

3   World War I took away about 5% of Europe's population.

In the aftermath of the Thirty Years' War, the Swiss Brethren moved north into Alsace and the Palatinate.

lands sometimes gave Anabaptists special deals because of their good work ethic. A few lords, being influenced by Pietism, were even sympathetic and turned a blind eye to the religious activities of their subjects.

Thus, while Jakob Ammann was still a lad, Anabaptists were beginning to trickle north out of Switzerland to the lands devastated by plague and war. Little did the lad realize he would someday follow and make his home in a small Alsatian valley.

Boom, then Bust

With every economic boom, a bust is bound to follow. So it was with the increase of money that circulated in the Swiss cantons during and immediately following the Thirty Years' War. An increase in available money means inflation. Rising incomes often mean more loans, since humans are prone to spend more than they have when times are good. Thus the poor—spiritually poor—Swiss were sucked into a waiting trap.

When the German states began recovering from the war, they no longer needed to import agricultural goods. Prices for grain and other commodities fell. Meanwhile, the cities in the Swiss Confederation had spent lots of money building fortifications and trying to be prepared in case the conflict would come to their land. The result was a big debt load, which they tried to overcome by raising taxes. When the Swiss mercenaries came home after the war, income from outside the cantons dropped. The sum total of all these factors was rising prices and falling income.

In response, Bern issued copper coins, called *Batzen*, that were by law valued the same as the silver coins that were previously minted. The rich tended to horde the silver coins, but the poor had no choice but to accept the copper coins in their transactions.

Then came the fateful decision: In December of 1652, the

To evangelize or not to evangelize?

A false story circulates in our day that the Swiss Anabaptist refugees signed contracts with the lords that accepted them onto their lands, agreeing not to evangelize. While a couple of extant documents show that this was part of their lease agreements, for the vast majority of cases this appears not to have been an explicit requirement. The fact of the matter was that in 17th-century Europe, open evangelism by Anabaptists was illegal everywhere. So when the Swiss Anabaptists settled in Alsace and the Palatinate, they did not sign agreements to not evangelize. They did, however, sign leases for certain buildings and fields that were owned by lords who forbade evangelism; but where could they have gone in Europe where evangelism was permitted? Nowhere! In today's world, it would be like an American missionary going to a foreign country to teach English. In their work contract, it would likely not specifically say that the missionary could not preach or teach Christian doctrine, but the laws of the land may prohibit that very thing.

Canton of Bern devalued the Batzen by 50%. This meant that the poor people, who used mostly the Batzen, suddenly lost half of their economic buying power.[4]

When the announcement was made for devaluation, everyone was given only three days to exchange the Batzen for silver or gold. This left the rural people stuck with the devalued coins, while the urban people who knew about the change had time to make the exchange. Enough was enough. The peasants arose in anger and began a revolution,[5] afterward called the Swiss Peasant War of

---

4   If a person was saving up to buy a product that cost 20 Talers (dollars), and had achieved 18 Batzen (with a Batzen equal to a Taler), when the devaluation occurred, he now only had the *equivalent* of nine Talers to buy the product still priced at 20 Talers.

5   During the Swiss Peasant War, the word "revolution" was used for the first time to describe

Pietism

As Anabaptism grew dramatically in Bern in the late 1600s, so did a new religious movement—Pietism.

Pietism began in the Lutheran churches of Germany. It focused on the need for people to experience the new birth, to live godly, righteous lives, and to receive edification from the teaching and preaching of God's Word. The movement was characterized by small group meetings (usually in homes) known as collegia pietatis, where people would gather to discuss scripture and receive edification.

There were two main groups of Pietists: church Pietists and radical Pietists. Church Pietists intended to bring renewal and reformation into the official Protestant churches. They thought that collegia pietatis gatherings, with renewed attention to edifying sermons and godly living, could accomplish this. Radical Pietists saw little good in the "Babylon" of the state churches, and left them altogether, finding their spiritual support and fellowship in the small Pietist gatherings.

Pietists tended to be critical of too-great attention to doctrinal subtleties. As a result, they were much more open-minded than many people of their age, and when Pietism spread to the Swiss Reformed lands, Pietists could have sympathy for persecuted Anabaptists despite their doctrinal differences. The government of Bern considered Pietism to be as much a threat as Anabaptism, and sought to suppress it.

1653. Jakob Amman was a boy when these country people rose up, just over the hills from his home, and tried to set up a government separate from the cities. The conflict was essentially a revolt of the

---

a social uprising.

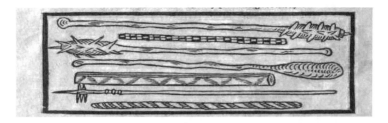

Weapons used by Bernese peasants in the Swiss Peasants' War.

country people against the city leaders, a rural vs. urban contest.

The revolt was quickly squashed, since the cities could afford

Niklaus Leuenberger, a leader in the Swiss Peasants' War.

to hire trained mercenaries who had cannons, while the peasants had few guns, and many were armed only with pitchforks and *Bauernknüttel*.[6] When the dust settled, the leaders of the revolt were rounded up and summarily executed. However, the city leaders began to be more considerate of the peasant population, realizing that if they imposed too many taxes, the people would again rise up in anger.

The main conflict played itself out in the rural areas between Bern and Zürich, with the Emmental—where many Anabaptists lived—being right in the middle of the action. This conflict brings to light how the common rural peasants often had no qualms with the Anabaptists who lived among them. They had more gripes against the cantonal government leaders who lived luxurious lives, all the while spitting out decrees and taxations for the people who did all the hard work. It is no wonder that some of the Anabaptists' neighbors took their side when canton officials

---

6   Clubs with nails sticking out of the hitting end.

would churn out another anti-Anabaptist decree!

The Little Ice Age

Besides being plagued with the Black Death and war, 17th-century Europe was passing through what is now called "the little ice age."[7] Global temperatures[8] seem to have dipped low, possibly causing shorter growing seasons in some areas, extending glaciers and the ice shelves around Iceland and Greenland, and in general making life just a bit harder in many parts of Europe.

Of course, Jakob Ammann probably had no idea that the earth was cooler than what had previously been "normal," but with conditions in Europe already gnarled by disease and war, having to deal with cold weather could only have furthered the miseries of the suffering poor.

---

7   Dates for the Little Ice Age vary, but in general the 17th and 18th centuries are the core of the varied dating schemes.

8   It needs to be understood that official temperature records were nonexistent, but by using clues from what was written (such as a certain river froze over completely on a certain date), and/or ice core samples from Arctic areas, researchers have reached their conclusions about the cooler temperatures of the era.

The Simmental Valley, where Jakob Ammann
was born and spent his boyhood.

CHAPTER 3

In Stockhorn's Shadow

akob Ammann first saw the light of this world among the pine-clad mountains, crystal-clear streams, and lowing cattle of the Simmental Valley just a few miles to the west of Lake Thun, Switzerland. If a man could live off of natural beauty, the residents of Erlenbach im Simmental[1] would be about as long-lived as anyone on this earth! What boy would not want to grow up with 7,190-foot Stockhorn Mountain in his backyard? This majestic masterpiece of God's handiwork is such a charming place that today a cable car has been built to access the summit. There, sitting amongst the clouds, one can eat at a restaurant while filling his soul with inspiration from the grandiose views. One has to wonder what young Yaggi Ammann would think to see a cable car floating over his home today![2]

---

1   "Bach" means creek, "im" means "in the," and "tal" means valley. Thus Erlenbach im Simmental is translated as Erlen Creek in the Simme Valley. Simmental cattle, known for their fast growth, were named after the Simme Valley, where they originated. At the head of the Simme River, just over the pass, lies the Saanen valley, from which Saanen goats received their name. Saanens are some of the biggest and best milking goats. Saanen goats and Simmental cattle give us a glimpse of the agricultural heritage of the area.

2   While the cable car does not pass exactly over the Ammann home, it would be clearly

Boys are boys and will always be boys. While we have no information about Jakob's childhood, it is hard to imagine that Jakob did not climb the Stockhorn with his brothers and the local boys. We can imagine Jakob and the neighborhood children clambering up the slopes of the pine-covered hills behind the house—and sliding down them in the winter on sleds of some sort. Wildenbach—Deer Creek[3]—spills down the hill a few hundred yards away, and hundreds of acres of forest lie just behind the house. A boy's delight!

The Ammann Clan

Jakob's grandparents were Uli and Catherina (Platter[4]) Ammann, to whom six children were born in Erlenbach. Jakob's father, Michel, was the fifth child, with a younger brother named Jakob. Grandpa Uli died less than one year after Uncle Jakob was born, with Michel being a lad of but three years of age.

Uncle Jakob had a son named Jakob, as well. Suffice it to say that Jakob Ammann was a common name in those days! "Ammann" is probably derived from the German word *Amptmann,*[5] which was a bailiff or sometimes similar to a small-town mayor. A bailiff is something akin to a sheriff's deputy, and we can imagine dozens of people serving as bailiff or mayor in medieval Switzerland. When men began to carry a last name, often based upon their occupation—think Miller and Baker and Smith—many different families could have taken on the last name of Amptmann or Ammann. Add to this the fact that Hans, Jakob, and Ulrich were very common first names in those days, and one can understand that family histories can get confusing very quickly!

---

visible about ½ mile away.

3   "Wilden" could refer to any wild game, but most often refers to deer.

4   Some spell it "Blatter."

5   Or, *Amtmann.*

Interior of the Erlenbach Reformed chapel, where Jakob Ammann was baptized as a baby on February 12, 1644.

Michel Ammann is recorded as being baptized—as an infant, of course—into the Reformed Church on August 18, 1615. He married Anna Rupp (baptized March 6, 1614) at Erlenbach on March 5, 1638. The couple's first child, a daughter named Madlena, was baptized on December 16, 1638. A son, Hans, followed in 1642.

Jakob Ammann was the third child and second son in the family. His Reformed Church infant baptism is recorded at the Erlenbach im Simmental chapel on February 12, 1644. Two more daughters entered the Michel Ammann family in Erlenbach: Cathrina (1647) and Anna (1651).

In 1655—when Jakob was around 11 years of age—the Michel Ammann family moved to Oberhofen, where the last known son joined the family. Ulrich (Ulli, for short) was born here and baptized on January 12, 1662, in the nearby Hilterfingen church. Jakob was nearly eighteen years old when his youngest brother joined the family.

That's too sumptuous!

It may not surprise you, but in the time of Jakob Ammann, a tailor got in trouble for making a pair of pants which were too fancy. What may surprise you is that it was not Jakob Ammann who thought that pants with a crease in them were too far out. Yes, it was the *Chorgericht*[1] of Aeschi—located less than 10 miles from Jakob Ammann's hometown of Erlenbach—that fined a tailor for making creases in pants for his customers.

Known as sumptuary laws, such restrictions were in place all across Europe. In an attempt to keep the serfs from thinking too highly of themselves, fancy clothes were restricted to only the nobility. Why, if a poor farmer put on some sumptuous clothing, he may just begin to think too highly of himself!

While it may seem outrageous to some people today to imagine that the clothes we wear affect our attitude, the reality is that the clothes we wear will often subtly change our feelings about ourselves. If you do not believe it, let a teenage boy pull on a pair of fancy cowboy boots, slip a Stetson hat on his head, and attire himself with a big belt buckle of a bucking bronco and see if he will not—even subconsciously—begin to swagger around like a real dude, thumbs hooked in his pockets.

Other motivations for sumptuary laws included a desire to prevent the common people from spending too much money on clothing and a desire to keep foreign clothing and fashions out of Switzerland.

Consider the following moral and sumptuary codes found in the Swiss cantons at one point or another.[2] Keep in mind that the Zürich

---

1   The *Chorgericht* were essentially morals courts closely aligned with the local church, enforcing morality codes such as those concerning Sunday activities, attendance at worship, clothing, and marriage.

2   John Martin Vincent, "European Blue Laws," *Annual Report of the American*

ordinance of 1628 begins with these words: "Since all mankind ought to seek the Kingdom of God. . ." And remember, these were not Anabaptist rules, but government laws!

- Jugglers, maskers, jumpers, and such like were forbidden, because they did things that God did not intend the human race to perform, and "are not allowed by the Christian religion."

- When the "bed bell" rang, all children were to be in bed or head there. Any child on the street after it rang could cost his parents a fine, or possibly a "pointed reproof" on how to raise children.

- No weddings were to be held on Sundays so that everyone could be in a church meeting. And, so as to keep people from getting too occupied in preparations that may hinder their church attendance, no weddings were to be held on Mondays. Saturday weddings were also prohibited, although the reason is not given.

- Unmarried girls could not ride on sleighs with any male except their father.

- The sale of playing cards was forbidden.

- Drinking wine was not forbidden, but in the evenings it was to be done only between 5 and 6 o'clock, with a strict prohibition against drinking in more than one place. People were not even allowed to drink once they reached home after drinking at a tavern.

- Weddings were not permitted to be larger than "six or eight" tables, with fewer recommended. Rural weddings were not supposed to have "the whole community" invited.

- No one was to take a walk in the fields on Sundays.

- Boys and girls were not permitted to walk the streets together.

Historical Association (1897):355-372.

- Clothes were not to be washed on Tuesdays so as to make sure that residents had plenty of time to attend the Tuesday evening church meeting.
- Public smoking of tobacco was forbidden.
- Lace and gold fringes were forbidden.

Jakob's father and grandfather were both tailors. "Like father like son" applied to Jakob as well, since he also pursued the same vocation.

How nice it would be to be able to peek into the thinking of someone from times past! Did Jakob look at his little baby brother and dream that one day they would both be ministers among the Swiss Brethren? Most likely not, since at this time the family appears to not have had any official relationship with the Anabaptists. Like almost everyone around them, they were Reformed Church members, whether serious about their religion or not.

On to Marriage

From all appearances, Jakob began married life sometime in the 1660s, marrying Verena Stüdler. Verena may have come from the village of Buchholterberg, about 10 miles north and east of Oberhofen, but we simply do not have clear information concerning her family.

In 1665, the Hilterfingen *Chorgericht* fined Verena because she "has carelessly brought fire and transported it without proper receptacles." With essentially all buildings made of wood, early modern Europeans had to be very careful about fire safety. Verena "asked for forgiveness and promised improvement," and the *Chorgericht*

This house, photographed about 1900, may have been the house in which Jakob Ammann grew up.

gave her a warning and a fine of five shillings.[6]

In November 1671, Jakob apparently needed cash, and so borrowed money from the poor fund. As security, he used a paid-off promissory note of his father's. While this could indicate the financial struggles of a young businessman, Jakob soon became a fairly successful tailor, economically speaking.

By May 1673, his parents were living back at Thal[7] and most of their children had left home. Jakob and Verena stayed on at Oberhofen. Michel and Anna contracted to pay their unmarried daughter Cathrina for taking care of them.[8] Michel was nearly 60

---

6   Hanspeter Jecker, "The Emergence of the Amish (1693ff.): Chronology and Background to the Collapse of an Ecclesial Transformation Process," *Mennonite Quarterly Review* 94(4) (October 2020):539-556, p. 549.

7   The old home place, one half mile above Erlenbach im Simmental.

8   Cathrina appears to have married Hans Schallenberg sometime before 1679. Hans is listed as in the Alsace in 1703.

Jakob Ammann grew to young manhood in Oberhofen on Lake Thun.

at the time.

Jakob seems to have remained faithful to the Reformed Church through the late 1670s. On March 12, 1671, he[9] served as a god-father or sponsor[10] at the baptism of Jacob Immer, son of Uli and Barbara (Frutiger) Immer. Today, these baptismal records help researchers decipher who lived where and who was related to whom.

All in all, Jakob appears to have had everything the world could offer to make him happy in the 1670s—a wife, perhaps children,[11] a good trade, a house, relative financial stability, and a state-approved

---

9   This could have been his uncle Jakob, since he lived in the area as well.

10   Acting as godparent originally meant that one was guaranteeing that the child would have good spiritual training, especially if the parents died.

11   The lack, thus far, of locating baptismal records of children born to Jakob and Verena does not indicate that he did not have any. The records could turn up any day now, they could be permanently missing, he could have had them baptized in a different village than thought, or he could have been on his journey toward Anabaptism and thus withheld baptism for his children. A later incident does show that he had at least one daughter.

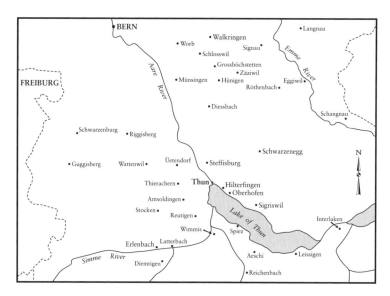

Jakob Ammann grew up and spent his young manhood in the Bernese Oberland near Lake Thun. Later, as an Anabaptist leader, most of his followers would also come from this region.

religion. But these things cannot satisfy the deepest longings of the human heart.

At some point, the Anabaptists and their beliefs began to draw his attention. How interesting it would be to know how that came about! His oldest sister, Madlena, had married Anthoni Wolff, and their oldest son, Hans, ended up among the Anabaptists in later years. The last names of Jakob's maternal grandparents, Hans Rupp and Madlena Frey, would become Anabaptist names which were transported to America. Who was the first to convert to Anabaptism? Who influenced whom? Dozens of families within a ten-mile radius of Jakob's home would eventually join the Swiss Brethren, abandoning the Reformed Church. The day came when Jakob himself had to choose to follow Christ—even though it meant living as a hated outlaw, a ridiculed Anabaptist, a hunted fugitive, and a fleeing refugee.

Had he been a serious Reformed Church believer beforehand? Or, as many in his day, did he just "put his time in" at so many church services each year so the *Chorgericht*, the "Morals Court," would leave him alone?

CHAPTER 4

Anabaptism Spreads Like Wildfire!

It may have been the strongest influx of fresh converts that the Swiss Anabaptist movement had seen since its beginning. How is it that over 200 new family names appear to be added to the Anabaptists in the space of about one generation—and all of them within what would be the size of one large county in the United States? The majority of modern Amish family names can be traced back to the brave souls who left the Reformed Church in Canton Bern in the 1670s-90s. Can we imagine 200 new Amish family names in the next 20 years, and all of them from one county? Anabaptism was truly spreading like wildfire—or, from the perspective of the Reformed authorities, like terrible invasive weeds.

Untold stories of faith and valor must have happened in those Alpine foothills. We will probably never know the details, because those who were acting as evangelists had to do so with greatest secrecy lest they be found out and imprisoned, or even killed. Most of what we know about the heroic nighttime meetings, the secret baptisms, and the hard choices to be true to God come from the

List of new Anabaptist names from the Bernese Oberland, late 1600s

Some of these names have changed forms slightly in North America.

Äbersold, Aeschbacher, Acherman, Albrecht, Algöwer, Alliman, Alwine, Ammann, Anken, Augsburger, Bächer, Bachman, Bäer, Baltzey, Barben, Baumgartner, Bauer, Bechler, Beck, Beieler, Bingelli, Blank, Blaser, Blassen, Blough, Bögli, Böller, Boshart, Brand, Bryner, Bucher, Bühler, Bürgi, Bütschi, Carli, Christener, Conrad, Dällenbach, Danner, Dätwyler, Ebersol, Eckhardt, Egli, Eimann, Engel, Erismann, Eyer, Fahrni, Feick, Fischer, Flückinger, Frey, Freyenberg, Frutiger, Furer, Galli, Gasser, Gäuman, Gautschi, Gehr, Gehrmann, Gerber, Gerig, Gindlesberger, Gisler, Glücki, Gnaegi, Goldschmid, Griesser, Grimstettler, Güngerich, Gurnter, Habegger, Häggi, Hauri, Haueter, Heineman, Heiser, Hersberger, Hirschi, Hodel, Hofer, Hoffman, Hofstettler, Holli, Hübscher, Hylti, Ingold, Im Hoff, Joder, Jordi, Jost, Jutzi, Kägi, Kämpf, Kaufmann, Kennel, Kilchhofer, Kisler, Kleiner, Klopfenstein, Kniep, König, Krähenbühl, Krämer, Krebs, Kropf, Kuenzi, Kunz, Kupferschmied, Kurtz, Lang, Lantz, Lapp, Lauffer, Lehmann, Lehner, Lengacher, Liechti, Linder, Litwiller, Lortschner, Luginbühl, Lutti, Martin, Mast, Maurer, Meister, Meyer, Mischler, Mosimann, Müller, Nafziger, Neuhauser, Nüssli, Oberli, Oesch, Ogi, Oswald, Peter, Petterschmied, Ranck, Ramsberger, Rapp, Reichenbach, Renold, Reusser, Rich, Richen, Richard, Riegsberger, Riehl, Ringgenberg, Roggi, Roller, Röschli, Roth, Rubi, Rüegsegger, Rupp, Sauder, Schaad, Schallenberger, Schantz, Schärtz, Schär, Scharpf, Schenk, Schlapach, Schlunegger, Schmidt, Schmucker, Schneider, Schrag, Schüppach, Schüpfer, Schwartz, Schwartzentrub, Schweitzer,

Schwaar, Seiler, Siever, Simon, Sommer, Sorg, Speicher, Springer, Stähli, Stalter, Steiner, Steinmann, Stöckli, Stoll, Stouffer, Streit, Strubhar, Stucki, Studer, Stutzmann, Sutter, Teuscher, Thoner, Trachsel, Treyer, Tschabold, Uli, Ummel, von Gunton, Vetter, Vordemwald, Wyse, Willi, Wittmer, Wolff, Würgler, Würtz, Zahler, Zehr, Zimmerman.[1]

---

1   List from Leroy Beachy, *Unser Leit*, 2011, Goodly Heritage Books, volume 1, pp. 116-117.

snippets of information found in records held in government archives. These records tell of Peter Roth, Hans Fahrni, and Yost Yoder taken to Bern for imprisonment, of Hans Kropf jailed in Thun for allowing Jakob Kaufman and his wife to stay at his house. Such records can only hint at what remained unrecorded.

Ulrich Müller, the Zealous Evangelist

One particular name stands out in the early years of the new growth of Anabaptism, that of Ulrich Müller. We know that other Swiss Brethren preachers were involved in spreading the movement, but at the time of this writing, Müller's ministry is the most documented by researchers. Court records show that at least eighteen people were given hefty fines for allowing "the criminal Anabaptist" Müller to stay or preach at their homes. Some of them spent many years paying off their fines, which amounted to up to two years of good wages—several years' wages if the person was making less.

Who was this Ulrich Müller? Since neither the preachers nor the listeners dared to keep records that could be found and used against them, and Social Security Numbers were unheard of at the time, we can only try to fit the puzzle together. One theory puts Ulrich as one of several Anabaptist Ulrich Müllers from Zürich, who, having been chased out of that canton—along with practically all the Anabaptists there—settled in the Aargau, on the north side of Canton Bern. From this base in Aargau, Müller then made many 40-mile evangelistic trips to the Lake Thun area, preaching and baptizing new converts. This theory of Müller is based largely on the fact that one court document from his later years shows that Müller was "von Hirschtal" (of Hirschtal), which is a town in Aargau.

The other theory of who this Ulrich Müller may have been is that he is one of four Ulrich Müllers who were born in Steffisburg in the 1640s. Several of the new converts to the Swiss Brethren were from the upper classes of the town, and Müller had some valuable properties there that were seized after he became an Anabaptist. If this is his real origin, he would have been a first-generation convert, a young man who in his 20s was risking his life running over the hills and preaching the gospel. He was arrested, and after his release[1] government records show that Müller lived in Alsace, where his first wife died during childbirth.[2] He then returned to the Steffisburg area, where he married a second time to a local woman. At this time, he would have been a hunted man who had already spent time in prison for his preaching. Thus, his later residence in Aargau may have been because he was chased out of Bern. After the mid-1680s, when Jakob Ammann was coming on the Anabaptist scene in Bern, Müller moved off to Alsace once again and the Bern court proceedings against him and those who housed him fall silent.

So which theory of Müller is correct? We do not know, and it is possible that more than one Anabaptist Ulrich Müller existed.

---

1   This may have been a forced exile, but that is only conjecture.

2   It seems that the child survived.

These theories are presented to show how complicated it can be to fit the historical pieces together into a complete picture.

Clash of Kingdoms

This tremendous advance against the kingdom of darkness was not without consequences. Attempts were made to squelch or restrict the movement, but they were stupendous failures. Despite Ulrich Müller and others being imprisoned, in these years the church was blessed with less stiff persecution than the Bern Council demanded. Some attribute this to the semi-tolerant *Schultheiss*[3] at Thun, Karl Manuel. He held office from 1686-1692 and may have obstructed the anti-Anabaptist efforts of the Reformed pastors and lower government officials in his territory. Although he was a fervent and pious churchman who was involved in bringing more than 200 Piedmont[4] Waldensian refugees to Thun—including semi-adopting one 15-year-old girl into his own family[5]—he was not entirely tolerant of Anabaptists. Records show his involvement in more than one imprisonment of Anabaptists. But there was another side to the story.

At church one Sunday, after the regular sermon, the preacher began to inform the congregants of the evils of the Anabaptists. At this point, Manuel simply asked the preacher to leave, and then turned to the waiting congregants. "One has to ask himself," he told them, "if the reason for all of our people leaving us and turning to the Anabaptists has to do with the failings of the preachers or not."

It is one thing if the common man in the pew murmurs and

---

3   A *Schultheiss* is a mayor, and in Thun he resided in the town castle. He has also been called a *Landvogt*, which is similar to a sheriff.

4   The Piedmont is an area of Italy where some of the last Waldensians had held out. As the crow flies, it is about 120 miles straight south of Lake Thun.

5   The girl, he wrote in his records, one day took off for the city of Bern by boat, "without reason and without saying goodbye" like a "light-minded and unthankful man."

The Castle of Thun. Karl Manuel, Schultheiss at Thun, was somewhat tolerant of the Anabaptists as they multiplied in the Bernese Oberland.

Wicked preachers

Karl Manuel of Thun was not the only Reformed person critical of the sinful lives of many of the Swiss Reformed clergy. In many government edicts regarding Anabaptism, the preachers with their sinful lives are blamed for causing people to leave the Reformed Church and turn to Anabaptism. In Steffisburg, which was near Thun and would later become a seedbed of the Amish movement, two Reformed preachers were particularly ungodly. One was beheaded for the lawless deeds of his youth, while his successor was fired for embezzlement and dull preaching—so dull in fact that it is said that a town official was the only person to attend his sermons!

complains behind the preacher's back, but it is another when the highest civil authority in town gives him a public slam! It is said that from that point on, the preacher simply had to be quiet about the Anabaptist "problem" in town until Karl Manuel's term as *Schultheiss* was over. So even though he did jail a few Anabaptists, Manuel's position appears to be that of a half-hearted persecutor of the "heretics." During his term, Anabaptism in the Steffisburg and Thun area reached its greatest height.

Jakob Ammann Converts to Anabaptism

Jakob Ammann himself seems to have thrown in his lot with the Swiss Brethren sometime in 1678 or 1679, but it is unknown if and for how long he may have been attracted to the movement beforehand. How, when, and from whom he heard the first Anabaptist sermon is one of the secrets of history that will probably never be known. Neither is it known how much Bible knowledge or religious training he had prior to his rebaptism. While some converted to Anabaptism from a life of open wickedness, others were sincere Reformed Church

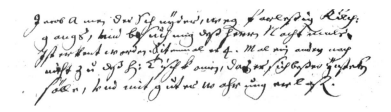

This entry in the records of the Hilterfingen Chorgericht, dated June 22, 1679, says that Jakob Ammann had been absent from the Lord's Supper in the Reformed Church four times.

devotees who got tired of hypocrisy in the state church.

Whatever may have been his attitude toward religion beforehand, court records show that in 1678 Jakob stopped attending the communion services of the Reformed Church. This made it hard for the preacher, who was supposed to inform the *Chorgericht* of straying church members if he could not get offenders to straighten up. So instead of the church disciplining erring members, the state was called in. Can you imagine a village policeman[6] knocking on your door, wondering why you have not been to a church meeting in a while?

By 1679, Jakob appears to have become a committed Anabaptist, and began making preparations to leave the area. Anabaptists who were caught by the authorities could have all their possessions confiscated. One of the anti-Anabaptist mandates even made it illegal to buy goods or land from an Anabaptist, and if one did so, the state could take them away from the new owner. Jakob most likely knew all of this. The law of the land was designed to trap them: If they kept their goods, the state could take them away. If they sold their goods, the state could take them from the new owner. In short, the law was really simple: If you become an Anabaptist, you lose everything, one way or the other! The only way out was to recant and turn back to the state church.

---

6   The *Chorgericht* were not policemen, but some have dubbed them "the morality police."

Sell that thou hast

Several years before Jakob Ammann became an Anabaptist and sold his house to his younger brother, a government official from Signau in Canton Bern wrote that such financial dealings were common practice among those leaving the state church and joining the Anabaptists:

> Furthermore, the practice of many of those who wish to join this sect has been to divide all, or most, of their property among their children under the guise of a bill of sale, trust agreement, or some type of provision before they commit themselves to Anabaptism. Thus they arrange that, after their death, nothing of their estate can be found and brought into the hands of Your Graces [the government].[1]

1   Ernst Müller, *History of the Bernese Anabaptists*, 2010 (originally published 1895), Pathway Publishers, p. 373.

On August 2, 1679, the government records show that "Master Jacob Amen the tailor, resident at Oberhofen" sold his house and vineyard to his younger brother Ulrich, who was eighteen years old at the time and was living at Thal near Erlenbach—probably with his parents. The purchase price was 1300 pounds.

Now here is where some fancy financial footwork begins. Ulrich agreed to pay the sum in installments spread over four years, with a down payment of 500 pounds. Jakob turned around and loaned most of this cash back out. Earlier in 1679, he had loaned 300 pounds to Ulrich Immer. Interestingly, one of the witnesses of this transaction was another Jakob Ammann, in all probability his uncle. With his new supply of cash, it is recorded that between November 11, 1679 and January 1, 1680, he loaned out a bit over

500 pounds to three different people. One of them was a Stüdler, very likely a relative of his wife. Another was Hans Schallenberg, who later ended up as his brother-in-law.

From all appearances, Jakob was making some financial preparations for what he probably knew was coming: confiscation of his goods if he was discovered to be an Anabaptist. Ulli, to whom he sold his house, was not yet of legal age (a few months shy of 18), and was not known to be Anabaptist yet. If authorities tried to confiscate Jakob's goods, the house would be in the name of his younger brother, who was a minor. This would probably cause the authorities to back off from taking it. If they went for Jakob's money, it was all loaned out, even though most of it was to relatives.

A Special Deal?

We do not know what was going on behind the scenes with these arrangements. But if we read between the lines, the dealings were probably a way that he could escape the land and later have the money sent to him.

We must remember, though, that we are only surmising about what may have been going on. Whatever happened, during the 1680s and 90s, dozens of Anabaptist families from the Steffisburg/Thun area emigrated (or were forced) out of Bern. Many of them, like Jakob Ammann, ended up in the Alsace. Here, the climate was very similar and the hills may have made the former Alpsmen feel somewhat at home.

Jakob is Found Out

In 1680, the governor of Oberhofen, apparently not knowing what to do with Jakob, wrote to the *Chorgericht* in Bern for information on how to deal with "Jacob Amman of Erlenbach" who was now "infected by the Anabaptist sect." Anabaptist affairs were

The Council's answer

From the request delivered to the Chorgericht by him[ambiguous], and which has also been forwarded to Your Grace, and you have seen yourself, to what extent Jacob Amman of Erlenbach has let himself be infected by the Anabaptist sect: concerning the requested direction, your Graces advised to summon him for a deposition and through friendly admonition, by yourself as well as by the preachers, to use diligence to bring him back to the right way: if he says he agrees, then good!; if not, he shall be led to the border and be banished from the country, with the understanding that even if he will not swear the oath, reentering the country will result in punishment with rods as a perjurer and expulsion. He shall then inventory his possessions, divide it with the children. The father's portion shall be put into the care of the church steward, according to the Anabaptist mandate. But in case he does not have the mandate, he should apply for it at the government office, either get a written copy or have it explained to him by some person.[1]

---

1   Mark Furner, "On the Trail of Jacob Ammann," *Mennonite Quarterly Review* 74(2) (April 2000):326-328, p. 328; translated by John B. Martin and Isaac Lowry.

usually handled by each locale's *Chorgericht*, but major cases were referred to the central authorities. The *Chorgericht* in the city of Bern (the seat of the cantonal government) was an appeals court for the rest, thus the governor's inquiry was directed to it.

How did they find out Jakob had turned Anabaptist? We do not know, but most likely the local minister in the state church was keeping records of who showed up for communion and preaching.

On June 4, 1680, the Council of Bern itself replied to the Oberhofen governor's question. The Council gave the standard orders: Jakob should be summoned for questioning and the local Reformed pastors should try to persuade him to recant. If he refused to recant, he should be escorted to the border of the canton and told to swear an oath to never return to the canton. If he refused to swear, he would be informed that if he returned, he would be considered a perjurer and flogged. Upon banishment, his property should be confiscated and distributed to his children.

There is no record of any further legal action taken against Ammann in Oberhofen. It is possible that the delay necessitated by the governor's ignorance of the Anabaptist laws gave Jakob enough time to escape from Oberhofen. If he had already disposed of his real estate, he only had to pack his bags and go. How, when, and where he left Bern still remains one of those hidden secrets of history. Researchers are still digging in the archives, but we likely will never know the full story. We only know that more than a decade later he was living in the Alsace. At some point, his youngest brother Ulrich also joined the Anabaptists.

The only little peek into Jakob's life that we have in that decade occurred in 1690, when he made a visit to Steffisburg, most likely a pastoral or evangelistic tour. Some non-Anabaptist women happened upon a meeting which Jakob held in Steffisburg and were later questioned by the authorities about their involvement. Jacob Engemann's wife, from Thun, reported to the authorities, upon being questioned:

> It is true that she visited a house at Steffisburg with which she was not familiar. Some people were assembled there, but she had

nothing to do with them. She was in the company of the wives of Mr. Lantzrein and Rudolphe Stähli. The house is located opposite the inn and belongs to someone named Joder. There she spoke with Jaggi Amann, an Anabaptist, and listened to what he had to say. But the three women had not gone to that place for that reason. It was a Sunday, after the prayer service. The three women spoke with Amann about the sect, and she herself engaged in conversation with him. . . .[7]

The lady supposedly just listened to what Jaggi had to say, but she certainly had *not* gone to the Anabaptist meeting on purpose, she claimed. Her claim may be true, but it smells of someone who is making excuses. If she admitted to going to an Anabaptist meeting on purpose, a hefty fine would probably be levied against her. Whatever the case, it appears that by 1690 Jakob was preaching.

We know that at some point Jakob was ordained to the ministry, and eventually became a bishop. Who ordained him? An undated letter by a certain David Baumgartner states: "It was this Hans Reist who had ordained Jacob Ammen and charged him with ministry."[8] However, because the letter is undated, we do not know exactly who this Baumgartner was, and if his information is fact or hearsay. Ulrich also was eventually ordained.

The name Hans Reist brings us to the next part of Jakob's life, for which we have much more information, including letters written by him. But before we look at this, it is needful to back up once again and consider the Swiss Brethren church to which Jakob had attached himself.

---

7   Robert Baecher, "From Steffisburg to Ste. Marie-aux-Mines: The Exodus of Those Who Would Become Amish, Part II," *Mennonite Family History* 23(2) (April 2004):69-81, p. 81.

8   John Hüppi, "Identifying Jacob Ammann," *Mennonite Quarterly Review* 74(2) (April 2000):329-339, p. 336.

Dutch & North German Anabaptists

1531	**1534-35**	**c. 1536**
Melchior Hoffman	Münster Rebellion	Menno Simons
begins Anabaptism in Holland		ordained

Swiss Brethren

ZÜRICH

1525	**1527**	**1614**
First	Schleitheim	Hans Landis
baptisms	confession	martyred

BERN

1526
Anabaptism
introduced

This timeline shows some of the major events and personalities mentioned in this book, placing them in their Anabaptist context. It shows
the relationship between the Dutch/North German Mennonites and
the Swiss Brethren.

c. 1561
Menno dies

Mennonites
fracture

1632
Dortrecht
Confession

— **1640s**
Anabaptism
exterminated

ENTAL

1670-90
New outbreak of
abaptism in Oberland

1693-94
Reist Ammann

1695
Oberland
Anabaptists
to Alsace

1711
Anabaptist
exodus

The Swiss Brethren faced persecution from their beginning in 1525 to long after Jakob Ammann's time. They scattered to the Alsace, Palatinate, and North America.

CHAPTER 5

The Swiss Brethren

arlier in the story we alluded to the beginnings of the
Swiss Brethren—which the Swiss Anabaptists tended
to call themselves—in Zürich in 1525.[1] Very shortly after that, evangelists from Zürich came to Bern, where a reform
movement was gathering momentum. At that time, Bern was still
Catholic, and only on February 7, 1528, did the Bernese authorities
decide to become Protestant. When the first Anabaptist evangelists
arrived in Bern, they found a radical reforming movement already
stirring and introduced the practice of believer's baptism.

The story from there to Jakob Ammann, 150 years later, is
one of suffering. Again and again the authorities would roll out
a new mandate of persecution, or renew an existing one. The
first Anabaptist blood spilled in Bern was only three years after the movement started, in 1528. From that point on, it was a
continuous up-down relationship. No, not a love-hate relationship, but a hate-tolerate—even though it was mostly a grudging

---

1   For a detailed account of the beginnings of Anabaptism, see Andrew V. Ste. Marie and
Mike Atnip, *March Forward with the Word: The Life of Conrad Grebel*, 2016, Sermon on the
Mount Publishing.

toleration—relationship.

Several times in the first decades, the authorities were "lenient" enough to try to debate with the Anabaptists, rather than just kill or banish them. But the Anabaptists soon tired of the theatrics; it did not matter what they said, they were always declared the losers. They finally quit responding to the invitation to another fruitless debate.

The Bern authorities, as just mentioned, at first executed some of the Swiss Brethren in 1528. But just three years later, in 1531, they began to loosen up a bit: now they "waterboarded" them. Actually, it was called "dunking," where they would stick the person's head in a barrel of water until he was almost dead, then quickly pull him out before he actually drowned. The human soul will naturally shrink in terror at almost drowning, and this form of torture is considered some of the worst psychological torture that exists.[2]

Two years later (1533), a broader toleration was offered: If the Anabaptists would keep quiet, attend church, and baptize their children, they would be spared their lives. This amounted to saying that rebaptism would be tolerated—if they would keep it solely to themselves. Suffice it to say that in those early days of the movement, this was unacceptable to most of the Swiss Brethren! Sure enough, just two years later, in 1535, another stricter mandate was given against them.

Then came about a rather strange situation. The Bern authorities sent a man named Hans Franz Nägeli over to France to try to persuade the Catholic French government to stop persecuting the Huguenots (French Protestants). It must have never occurred to

---

2   Readers may be aware that the U.S. government has been accused of using waterboarding even in the 21ˢᵗ century. We cannot, therefore, claim that the Bernese authorities were any more inhumane than modern people are.

them—at least they never mentioned it—that it was rather hypocritical to ask the French Catholics to stop persecution of their people, when they themselves were persecuting others!

But Nägeli returned home with a message for the Bernese authorities. In a meeting with them, he let them have it. The problem is, he said, that the preachers are living so ungodly that people are turning away from the state churches to the Anabaptists. It was, in fact, their own fault that people were abandoning the Protestant religion. And the problem was not just with the preachers, but with the civil authorities as well.

Bam! The speech had its effect. The very same day the Bernese authorities released a milder interpretation of the mandate against the Anabaptists. But it only lasted a short time; within three years Anabaptist blood was being spilled once again on Bernese soil by the authorities.

Like the hills and valleys of the canton, persecution and semi-tolerance went back and forth through the following decades. In 1566, a new mandate took a different approach. Since the Swiss Brethren refused to swear oaths because Jesus forbids such (Matthew 5:33-37, James 5:12), the authorities began to use this against them. Now, every man was required to come before the local authority and swear an oath of allegiance to the state, once every year. Authorities would take notice of anyone in the community who did not show up for these annual oaths, and this information was used to probe for Anabaptists in their midst.

In 1567, a new mandate was given that declared any marriage outside of the state church illegitimate. This meant that children from such a marriage could not inherit any property, and it gave grounds for the state to remove the children from the parents. The Anabaptists continued to perform their own marriages, recognizing that God makes marriages, not the state or its church.

In 1581, the authorities acknowledged again that sin in the clergy was one reason people were inclined to leave the state church. However, they still legislated punishment against the Anabaptists, this time either life in prison on a minimal diet, or banishment.

By August 1585, the authorities humbled themselves once again. A new mandate was sent forth, but this one included a reproof against the sin in the lives of the Reformed Church's preachers.

A dozen years passed. Once again, in 1597, the old mandate of 1585 was renewed, with the requirement that it be publicly read from every pulpit at least once a year.

Did this requirement backfire? Instead of stirring the people against the Anabaptists, reminding the state church attendees about the evils of Anabaptism may well have served to remind everyone that there was another option out there besides the lukewarm and sinful state church!

Back in Zürich

About a century had passed since Anabaptism was birthed in Zürich. On September 30, 1614, an old, long-bearded Anabaptist was beheaded in Zürich. Hans Landis, a minister, was respected by many people in the area as a godly man, and the reaction to his execution was enough to stop authorities in the canton from killing any more Anabaptists.

But not all was well among the Swiss Brethren. Several generations had passed since its founding, and, as is common among all religious revivals, some of the zeal had cooled off. Compromises were beginning to dull the once-sharp edge of truth that the early Anabaptists had dug out and burnished once again from the Bible. For instance, some Swiss Brethren were having their infants baptized. They would not take them to the state church preachers themselves, but would have friends and relatives take the babies for baptism for them. Conrad Grebel would have "turned over in the grave." He had refused to have his new baby girl baptized, at the risk of being kicked out of the city. The earliest Swiss Brethren and Anabaptists in other parts of Europe had used no uncertain terms to describe infant baptism: It was an "abomination," said some of them, something to be avoided at all costs. One early Anabaptist father washed his infant son after the baby had been baptized against his will![3] But now their descendants were compromising and allowing their babies to be baptized by the state church. Infant baptism was necessary for inheritance purposes, and this may have been the reason for the practice. Do material possessions give a reason to partake of an abomination? The first generation would have given a resounding "NO!"

How Far Gone?

All renewal movements grow cold after a while. Usually, the first generation is a group of firebrands and zealots for God and truth. This is what creates renewal: God has said that we would find Him when we seek Him "with all your heart."

But the generations following a renewal lose that zeal, some individuals faster, and some slower. By the time of Hans Landis' death, about three or four generations would have passed. Usually, each generation grows sleepier than the previous one, but within each of those generations there are often those, a minority, who try to fan the flames and stir things up again. We do not *know* that this is what happened in the Züricher Swiss Brethren, but we can see that same pattern all through history.

---

3   John S. Oyer, *They Harry the Good People Out of the Land*, 2000, Mennonite Historical Society, p. 301.

What about in Bern?

About ten years before Jakob Ammann was born, the canton
of Zürich—which had also persecuted Anabaptists severely at
times—again took stern measures against them. The pressure became so intense that practically all the Anabaptists from Zürich
finally left the canton for good. Anabaptism in Zürich simply died
out, to this very day.

Most of the refugees from Zürich ended up going north to
Alsace (now part of France) and the German Palatinate. A few
ended up in Bern.[4]

One of the immigrants to the Emmental from Zürich was
named Heinrich Funck. Some evidence indicates that "the upper
brethren"—those from around Lake Thun, Jakob Ammann's home
area—shunned Heinrich Funck for some reason, but the "lower
brethren" (from the Emmental) apparently did not.[5] This would
have happened *before* Jakob Ammann became an Anabaptist, possibly indicating that there were stress cracks in the unity of the Swiss
Brethren at least a decade before Jakob Ammann joined them.

Heinrich lived for about twenty years in the Emmental/Aargau[6]
area. One day his 18-year-old daughter took her infant child to
the Reformed Church to be baptized. This would have been, as
we looked at earlier, totally unacceptable in the first generation of
Anabaptists. (Of course, it is not known whether the girl claimed
to be an Anabaptist.) At the same time, it should also be noted that
Heinrich Funck himself had had six children baptized in the local

---

4   The valley of the Emme. This was just to the north and east of the Lake Thun area where
Jakob Ammann lived, with the closest areas of the Emmental being less than 10 miles from
Steffisburg.

5   Hanspeter Jecker, "Heinrich Funck—the Man Whom They Branded," in Urs B. Leu and
Christian Scheidegger (editors), *Die Zürcher Täufer 1525-1700*, 2007, Theologischer Verlag
Zurich.

6   Aargau bordered the lower Emmental, and was under the rule of Bern at that time.

Reformed Church. The local authorities later considered Heinrich an "Anabaptist teacher."

The *real* problem was that the girl was unmarried; she was not even married by the Anabaptists. At the child's baptism, she apparently named the father of her child. This, of course, would have been a scandal that would have been referred to the *Chorgericht*. When investigated, however, the named father claimed he was *not* the father. Meanwhile, under shady circumstances, *another man* was being offered a large sum of money if he would take responsibility for fathering the child!

The whole incident blew over rather quickly when the child died shortly thereafter, but it seems to have alerted the authorities that Heinrich Funck was living in their territory. He was captured, taken to the border of the canton, whipped, and branded. As a matter of standard procedure, most likely he was told that he would be killed if they caught him in the canton again.

Poor Heinrich wandered three days before he found someone to bandage his wounds. He ended up in Alsace, a near neighbor of Hans Reist, who was living there at the time. Hans Reist figures greatly in the story of Jakob Ammann, as we shall soon see.

Liars!

The whole situation with Heinrich's daughter's out-of-wedlock child was, or at least should have been, a real smudge on the testimony of the Bernese Anabaptists. These incidents show us that these men and women were human like the rest of us, not some super-group of people who had no failures among them. Did the "upper brethren's" shunning of Heinrich Funck have anything to do with his daughter's out-of-wedlock child and the shadowy suggestion that someone was trying to pay off a man to take responsibility for fathering it? The question remains unanswered. The fact

Probier-Stein

Do not forget that there are two sides to every story. The Bernese Anabaptists may indeed have been losing their zeal and compromising in some areas, but nevertheless, there is clear evidence that they continued to leave a good testimony to their neighbors.

This evidence comes in the form of a book by a Reformed pastor published in 1693—the very year of the beginning of the Amish dispute. The Bernese government wanted a book to be written refuting Anabaptism, and George Thormann rose to the challenge. Writing in German, he produced an over 600-page book titled *Touchstone [Probier-Stein], or Most Certain Examination of Anabaptism, from Scripture and True Inner Christianity.*

The book was not bitterly critical of the Anabaptists, as many earlier Protestant books had been; in fact, in some ways it was complimentary. Thormann recognized that the Anabaptists enjoyed an extremely good reputation among the Bernese people. He said that many "look upon them [the Anabaptists] as holy, as salt of the earth, as the truly chosen race, and the heart of all Christians. . . many think, that a good Christian and a *Täufer* [literally Baptist, referring to the Anabaptists] are one. And one can hardly be a good and true Christian except he is or becomes a *Täufer*."[1]

Thormann did not write to convince Anabaptists to come back to the Reformed church; rather, he wrote to convince Reformed readers attracted to Anabaptism that it was not only unnecessary to become an Anabaptist to be saved, but was actually dangerous. One of his main arguments was that Christians should obey the government, and the government had mandated Reformed religion. Furthermore, the Anabaptists had, in his opinion, no valid reason to separate from

---

1   George Thormann, *Probier-Stein*, translated by Katharina Epp, 2005, pp. 75-76.

the Reformed church.

Thormann's book reveals that the Swiss Anabaptists were still leaving a good testimony to those around them, and the Reformed church and government considered them enough of a threat to devote 600 pages to trying to keep their members from joining the Anabaptists!

that some Swiss Brethren shunned him, however, while others did not, seems to indicate that views on church discipline were already diverging before Ammann joined them.

But that was not all that was happening in the Emmental. One Emmental state church preacher reported that he went to visit a man that he knew—or at least suspected—was an Anabaptist. When he arrived at the man's residence, the man's wife informed him that the man was not at home because he had gone to town.

However, about that time—not knowing that his wife had just reported him as gone off to town—the man stepped out of the cellar! He had heard the preacher's voice, and when he realized who it was, he had decided he would like to talk to him.

Oops! Was this an accident, a misunderstanding? Had the wife really thought that her husband had gone to town?

That could be the case, but the preacher left the visit with the idea that the woman had simply lied. Lied, plainly and openly.

Again, one may ask how this incident ties in with Jakob Ammann, but in just a few pages we will see that one of the issues that Jakob had against Hans Reist was that a woman who admitted she had told a lie had not been disciplined by the church.

This may not be the case to which Jakob was referring, but these two incidents, recorded by people outside of the Swiss Brethren churches, give us a sense that maybe things were not going so well in Emmental Anabaptism. On the other hand, even in churches that are thriving overall, there are always failures that happen along the edges.

Were the Emmental Anabaptists slipping into lukewarmness? They probably did not see it that way. They had been battling for survival for nearly two centuries, and had hung on to existence. To them, a compromise here or there—such as having their babies baptized—might have been seen as justifiable if it helped them survive. To at least some of the Oberlander Anabaptists, it also appeared that the church's discipline of those who had fallen into sin—particularly the sin of lying—was slipping seriously.

In Alsace, there were other indications of laxity, particularly attendance at meetings of the state church (about which we will see more in the next chapter). The Anabaptists there, most of them descendants of the Zürich refugees, lived in an atmosphere of religious toleration and some were assimilating into their environment.

These kinds of compromises and evidences of lukewarmness bothered the Oberlander Anabaptists greatly. What they did about their concerns led directly to the first major church split among the Swiss Anabaptists.

Lukewarmness can enter any renewal movement, even the hottest of them. We dare not relax in the war against it, lest we become the next casualty of carelessness!

There was a man named Jakob Ammann who came to the opinion that the true Christian discipline had been lost to a certain extent and resolved that he wanted, according to his thinking, to rebuild the temple of God on the old foundations. He especially promoted a doctrine regarding the shunning of those who had been banned in which he wanted that the banned person should be avoided in physical and spiritual meals. . .

Thereupon, the people split into two parts, and as a consequence thereof, many discussions were held with each other but no good fruit seemed to grow out of it.

—Anonymous Reistian copyist (?c. 1694)

Roth, p. 49

CHAPTER 6

Has Discipline Been Lost?

e are now arriving at the epoch in Jakob Ammann's life that has defined his reputation as a hard-headed, presumptuous dictator. Indeed, the decade beginning in 1693 provides us with the bulk of information that we have about him, including the only surviving writings that he composed.

But we have to back up one more time to see the whole picture of what brought about the so-called "Amish Division." In fact, we have to back up all the way to the beginning of the Anabaptist movement, but this time, we need to look at earliest Anabaptism in the Netherlands, rather than in Zürich.

Melchior and Menno

The first recorded rebaptism in the Anabaptist movement took place in Zürich in 1525, as we have already noted. From there, the practice spread, within just a few years, to most of German-speaking Europe. However, the desire to reform and revive the Catholic Church had been fermenting long before 1525, and in practically all of Europe. In Holland, reforming ideas were percolating in groups like the Brethren of the Common Life and among individuals as well. A furrier by the name of Melchior Hoffmann, born about 1495 in Schwäbisch-Hall in Germany, began to seek for reform as a young man. He associated with some Anabaptists in the German city of Strasbourg, but what brought Hoffmann his claim to fame was that he traveled north into Holland and began to preach and practice rebaptism there. Thus he is called, by some, the "father of Dutch Anabaptism."

Melchior was certainly not Swiss Brethren, and he had some very strange ideas. He was attracted to prophetic utterances and speculative ideas about end-times prophecy. He ended up in prison in Strasbourg after claiming that Jesus was going to return and set up His kingdom, with the center of that kingdom in Strasbourg. Melchior also made some prophecies concerning this, which did not come to pass. In short, he proved himself to be a false prophet. He died in prison in Strasbourg.

Some of Melchior's ideas provided the foundation for the debacle called the Münster Rebellion, in which men who had been rebaptized—and thus were considered "Anabaptists"—took over the city of Münster and claimed that Jesus was going to return and set up His kingdom there. Their message was essentially a version of Melchior's ideas, but they changed the location of the chief city of the prophesied kingdom and added the idea that Christians should use military tactics to inaugurate God's kingdom—something Melchior Hoffman had not promoted.

The whole thing turned exceedingly sour when the Münster Anabaptists took up arms to defend themselves, and meanwhile began practicing polygamy and other carnality. It was a royal mess, indeed! The city was recaptured by civil authorities, and the leaders of the rebellion were executed.

About the time Münster fell, a man named Menno Simons converted to Anabaptism. But Menno was of a different stripe than Melchior, even though he most likely heard the Anabaptist message first through some Melchiorites. Menno was able, along with several other Dutch Anabaptists, to gather together a sizable group of Dutch Anabaptists that was very similar to the Swiss Brethren. These "Mennonites," as they later came to be called, held to nonresistance, non-swearing of oaths, and separation of church and state.

Mennonite Splits and Splinters

Most Anabaptists in the earliest days of the movement believed that God's church was to be pure, but the Dutch Mennonites emphasized purity more than some other Anabaptists. This strong emphasis on church purity is probably one of the reasons that Dutch Anabaptism suffered from serious splits and splinters, from the very first generation. There were long and sharp arguments among the Dutch over small details of theology. Some of the Dutch said that there is only one true church, and that there can be only one particular Confession of Faith that every person must agree with in every fine detail. Those who disagreed were excommunicated.

One major area of dispute among the Dutch Anabaptists was how much to shun, or avoid social contact with, those who had sinned and refused to repent, and therefore had to be put out of the church. Specifically, what did Paul mean when he wrote about an excommunicated person, "with such an one no not to eat" (I Corinthians 5:11b)? The Swiss and South German Anabaptists, for the most part, believed that Paul was referring to the eating of Communion, while most of the Dutch Anabaptists said that it meant "to eat common meals," but they disagreed with each other over how to practice such shunning between marriage partners. Menno Simons wrote:

We reply, moreover, that Paul had reference to common eating, and not to the Lord's Supper. . . if this were spoken of the Lord's Supper, as some very ignorantly assert, then it would incontrovertibly follow that we are at liberty to invite the world to the Lord's Supper, to greet them with the kiss of peace, and to be one body with them; for this intercourse, unclean and prohibited with an apostate brother, is, according to Paul, clean and permissible with the world. Oh, no![1]

Healing Schism

In 1627, some ministers among the divided Dutch Anabaptists met together to seek for a healing of the schisms. Putting their heads and hearts together, they wrote a common Confession of Faith, now referred to as the Olive Branch Confession, which did bring about a merger between a few of the churches. In 1632, another similar attempt was made between the two main groups of Flemish Mennonites. The resulting Confession was signed by 51 Dutch Anabaptist ministers from the two groups. Since the confession was written in the city of Dortrecht, it is usually referred to as the Dortrecht Confession of Faith.

On the issue of shunning, the Dortrecht Confession teaches a complete social shunning, but "moderation and Christian discretion must be used." No specifics are given as to what that means, but it does leave the possibility of allowing married couples to have a normal married life, in the name of moderation and discretion. On the other hand, for those who still felt that shunning included marriage relationships, the Confession did not prohibit such.

1   "A Clear Account of Excommunication," in J. C. Wenger, editor, *The Complete Writings of Menno Simons*, 1984, Herald Press, p. 474. © Herald Press. Used with permission. All rights reserved.

The Dortrecht Confession Spreads to the South

In 1660, twenty years before Jakob Ammann converted to Anabaptism, the Dortrecht Confession was signed in Ohnenheim, Alsace—the area where Jakob would later live—by six ministers and seven deacons of the Züricher Swiss Brethren, accepting it "as their own." However, they must have done so either without fully understanding what the confession said about shunning or with mental reservations about what it said. This is demonstrated by the fact that Rudolph Egli, one of the Swiss Brethren ministers who had signed his agreement to the Dortrecht Confession, also "spoke strongly against shunning" sometime before the Amish Division.[2] The same Confession of Faith was later given to the Bern authorities by some Swiss Brethren as an official statement of what they believed.[3] In 1692, the Bernese government forbade possession or distribution of the Dortrecht Confession.[4]

Not all the Swiss Brethren may have been aware of these events. These were not brotherhood-wide decisions, especially the signing in Ohnenheim.

Why Does This Matter?

The Dortrecht Confession contained a couple of elements that were new to the Swiss Brethren. While the Swiss had always taught the excommunication of unrepentant sinners from their congregations, the issue of how to manage social shunning seems never to have been practiced uniformly. Some practiced social

---

2   Jakob Gut, "Jakob Gut to Peter Lehman and Rudolf Hauser," in John D. Roth, *Letters of the Amish Division: A Sourcebook*, 2nd edition, 2002, Mennonite Historical Society, (cited hereafter as Roth), p. 104.

3   Ulli Ammann, "Summary and Defense," in Roth, pp. 92-93.

4   Roth, p. 93, n. 29.

shunning, while many did not.[5] The degree to which shunning should be practiced seems to have been left up to the discretion of each congregation.

Another teaching of the Dortrecht Confession that was new to the Swiss was the washing of feet. The Swiss Brethren had never held that washing feet was an "ordinance" as such; they would have held to the idea that Jesus meant to teach a practice of humbly serving others, similar to the way that "taking up the cross" is viewed: Jesus did not mean for cross-bearing as an "ordinance" to be physically observed.[6] With this background in mind, we now proceed to the early 1690s, to Alsace. Here we find Jakob Ammann, who had emigrated out of Bern at an unknown date.

Bump in the Road

The first rumbles of possible trouble around Jakob Ammann began when Jakob and his congregation began to practice Communion twice a year instead of the traditional once-a-year observance. Why they introduced this change is not known. One Amish oral tradition holds that Ammann was motivated by the fact that expectant women in the congregations sometimes had to skip communion. For some, this could have happened several years in a row. With two communion services a year instead of one, they were given more opportunity to participate.[7]

---

5   Ulli Ammann wrote: "Several, however, who confessed shunning with us in the first conversation and said that there were plenty of scripture passages in favor of it, practiced shunning themselves. Later, however, when they saw that Hans Reist and others also did not want to support shunning but spoke strongly against it, they then drew back again from their confession and [the fact] that they had practiced shunning themselves and opposed it like the others" (Ulli Ammann, "Summary and Defense," in Roth, p. 84).

6   The Hutterites, an Anabaptist group which practices community of goods, have never taken up feetwashing as an ordinance, to this day.

7   Leroy Beachy, *Unser Leit: The Story of the Amish*, 2011, Goodly Heritage Books, Volume 1, p. 66. It is to be noted that this is an oral tradition that does not have any original source to verify it. Sometimes later generations make a guess as to why their forefathers did something,

This innovation caused some questions among the Anabaptists of the Emmental. When asked about the idea of holding communion more frequently, ministers Hans Reist and Benedict Schneider said that two times was no problem if the partakers were spiritually prepared for it. On the other hand, once a year was also sufficient—if the partakers were spiritually prepared. The main issue to them, it seems, was being prepared, not the number of times it happened per year. They upheld their traditional once-a-year position by noting that the Passover only occurred once a year.[8]

Although this innovation was a bump in the road, the bump ended up being only a bump and not a full-blown argument, since Jakob and his congregation did not expect every congregation to conform to their new practice. In this matter, Jakob and his congregation practiced the more Swiss style of church relationship, where minor details were not expected to be uniform across the brotherhood. For the Dutch, who wanted all things uniform, this may not have been allowed.

No Compromise Allowed

Meanwhile, back in Alsace, Jakob Ammann was confronting some of his Anabaptist neighbors about compromise. Living at Markirch (also known as Ste. Marie-aux-Mines) was a group of Swiss Brethren who had been in the area many years before Jakob and his newly-converted Oberlanders[9] arrived as immigrants.

The ministers there, Rudolf Hauser and Peter Lehman, were

---

and the guess becomes "fact" that is passed on through the generations.

8   Peter Giger, "Summary and Defense," in Roth, p. 19.

9   Oberlander means "high-lander" and was a term used to identify the brethren who had originated from around Lake Thun, which is higher up in the mountains than the Emmentalers. In some documents of that time, the "Amish" were called "Oberlanders" since the official division had not yet occurred, yet two diverse groups of Swiss Brethren were evident: the older lowlanders (from Zürich and the Emmental) and the newer, recently converted, highlanders.

allowing their congregants to attend services in the state churches. This caused the newer converts much concern. How could they act as if an apostate church that openly disobeyed Jesus was a good place to be fed spiritually? Jakob visited these lukewarm Anabaptists at least twice and tried to convince them that it was inappropriate to hear the preaching of the Pharisees, the ones who maybe said some good things, but did not do what God said to do. Hauser and Lehman, however, appealed to old custom[10] and said they did not want to deviate from it. With the counsel and approval of the ministers and elders, Ammann excommunicated those who refused to abstain from attendance at the state church.[11]

Rumors from the Heartland

At some point, Jakob and his fellow-ministers began hearing rumors coming out of the Emmental about Anabaptist ministers. These stories aroused concern in their hearts for the purity of the church. First, they heard that every minister practiced what he wished regarding shunning the excommunicated—there was no uniform practice and all seemed to do something different.[12]

Why the Oberlanders felt that there needed to be exact uniformity in this issue is not known. As noted earlier, from the beginning of the Swiss Brethren movement, no uniform practice had ever been officially established. We can probably assume that

---

10   It is unknown what "old custom" to which they were referring. This implies, however, that they had been attending the state church services for years or decades. This attendance may not have been regular, but perhaps enough to keep them out of trouble with the authorities.

11   Jakob Ammann, "Summary and Defense," in Roth, pp. 39-40. This may have occurred *after* Ammann's trip through Switzerland, although it seems unlikely. Ammann did not mention the names of those from Markirch whom he excommunicated, and it has been suggested that they were members of Ammann's own congregation. However, it was more likely to be someone from Hauser's congregations because this happened before November 1693 (when Jakob wrote about the event) and the Markirch Amish congregation did not exist until 1695, although Ulrich Müller did live there at the time.

12   Christian Blank, "Summary and Defense," in Roth, p. 114.

Three sects

As Ammann's confrontation with the Hauser/Lehman group in Markirch demonstrates, the Swiss Brethren were not all alike. The Zürichers, the Emmental Bernese, and the Oberlander Bernese Swiss Brethren had differences which led to the stresses resulting in the Amish division. In 1702, after an Amish group was established in Markirch, a Catholic priest by the name of Antoine Rice wrote the following description of the three Anabaptist groups in the area:

There are in Sainte-Marie-aux-Mines Anabaptists who are divided in three different sects and have no communication with each other as far as their religion is concerned. To distinguish among themselves, the men in one group have a long beard and the men and women wear clothing made only of linen cloth, summer and winter. In the other group the men have shorter beards and everyone dresses in coarse cloth; and the third group is about like the Catholics. These Anabaptists have no church building but meet in one of their homes (each one in his sect) which are often scattered in the mountains. Here they discuss their affairs and matters of religion and anyone is permitted to bring a message from the Word. [1]

Ammann's group was the long-bearded, linen-wearing group. The others are probably the Hauser/Lehman group (Zürichers whose parents had come to Alsace) and a group of Reistians from Bern.

---

1   Robert Baecher, "The 'Patriarche' of Sainte-Marie-aux-Mines," *Mennonite Quarterly Review* 74(1) (January 2000):145-158, pp. 150-151.

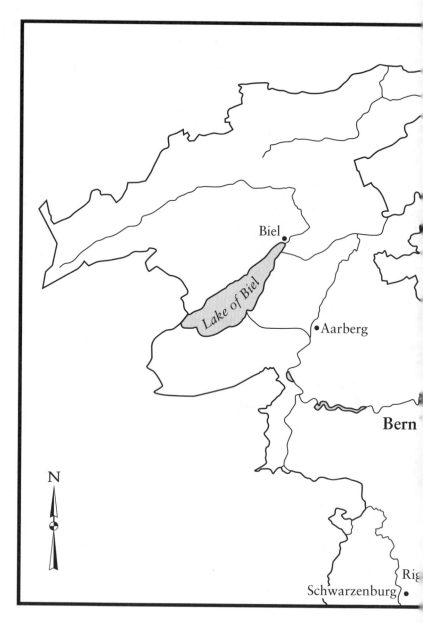

The Emmental area of Canton Bern along the Emme River. Steffisburg, at the bottom of the map, is north of Lake Thun, the Oberland area where Ammann and many of his supporters came from.

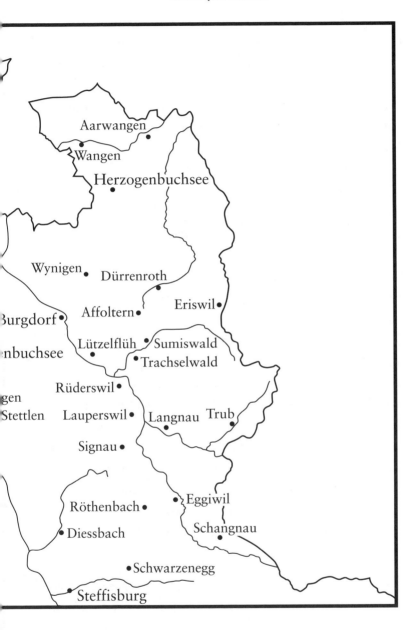

Dutch ideas of church administration may have been creeping in.

Secondly, there were rumors that some of the ministers in the Emmental were consoling the Truehearted and telling them that they were saved because of their good deeds toward the Anabaptists.[13] These "truehearted" people were also called *"Halbtäufer,"* which means half-Anabaptist. These "truehearted" agreed with the Anabaptist teachings and even risked their own safety to support and help the Anabaptists—for example, hiding them from officials sent out to arrest Anabaptists (some of the Truehearted were themselves government officials[14])—but they were unwilling to take up Jesus' cross by being baptized and joining the persecuted brotherhood. After all, open identification with Anabaptism meant possibly losing everything one had, possibly even one's life.

Jakob Ammann was indignant at the very suggestion of consoling the Truehearted with salvation. Remember, he was a convert from the state church—he was not brought up in the Anabaptist church. He was surrounded by many who had made the same decision he had—to leave everything behind, even the security of the state church, and take up the cross with the Anabaptists. Could there be a less demanding way? Could he give his blessing to those who halted between two opinions? Did the Scriptures teach that those who were unwilling to follow Christ all the way should be consoled in their non-commitment? Jakob wrote:

> There is only one faith that is valid before God, there is only one people who are the bride of Christ. Are we not among these people? Do we not have this faith? And if we do not travel along this path,

---

13   Ibid.

14   Ernst Müller, *History of the Bernese Anabaptists*, 2010 (originally published 1895), Pathway Publishers, p. 373.

even though it is narrow, then we cannot come to life. . . . in this way we may surely conform to God's Word and say: If a miser does not turn from his selfishness, and a fornicator from his fornication, and a drunkard from his drunkenness, or other immoralities, [they are] thereby separated from the Kingdom of God, and if he does not improve himself through a pious, penitent life, such a person is no Christian and will not inherit the Kingdom of God. . . . For we know well that God saves no one apart from His Word, for it is truth and there is no lie in it. Where there is no faith, no new birth or rebirth, no penance and improvement, over these Christ has already passed judgment, for He says: If you do not believe that I am the One, then you will die in your sins.[15]

It is important to note that Jakob did not teach that the Truehearted were necessarily unsaved; rather, he pointed out that they could not be consoled as "saved" when they had not taken up the cross of Christ, received believers' baptism, and joined the brotherhood. His brother Ulli acknowledged that they may have made a beginning in the Christian life, but they needed to be exhorted to continue—not be comforted in their lack of commitment. Additionally, Jakob did not ask anyone to shun or avoid the Truehearted; he only asked that the churches teach the truth about salvation as it related to the Truehearted. There is a fence, as it were, between death and life, but there are no riders on that fence. Either you are alive in Christ or dead in sins. Instead of seeing how close you can come to the fence and still be alive, God would have us move as far away from it as possible!

---

15   Jakob Ammann, "Summary and Defense," in Roth, pp. 34-35.

Other Truehearted

The Truehearted, or "half-Anabaptists," were actually a diverse group of people. They filled a spectrum of attitudes from those who actively supported the Anabaptists without joining them to those who simply attended an Anabaptist meeting or two, motivated by little more than curiosity.

A letter from a Dutch Mennonite describing the persecution of the Swiss Brethren in 1708 mentions one kind of Truehearted—people who attend Anabaptist meetings for spiritual benefit, but with no intention of joining the Anabaptists. He also mentions the high number of people who were converting from the state church to Anabaptism. This was one reason, he said, that the government persecuted the Anabaptists.

> . . . it is the case that the friends' meetings (which have to take place secretly at night) attract many visitors from the state church—to such an extent that many people, even those who have no intention of leaving the state church, appear there, with the intention and confidence that, through what is told there, they can give up some things to which they are strongly attached and in that way improve their [spiritual] lives. Since one finds also some who go further, and try to separate from the state church, this causes great hatred and bitterness, all the more because this happens a great deal and often. I have been told that once eighteen had come to the congregation, among whom there was no one but those from the state church.[1]

---

1   Jan Freriksz to Hermannus Schijn, January 6, 1708; translation from James W. Lowry, editor, *Documents of Brotherly Love Volume II*, 2015, Ohio Amish Library, p. 27.

Some "half-Anabaptists" were even less committed. In 1667, an Anabaptist meeting was held in Dürrenroth soon after the appearance of a comet in the night sky—understood by European commoners as a threatening omen. The meeting was thronged with visitors—so many that a large number of them could not hear what the preacher was saying. One man reported that he had to watch out to make sure no one stole anything from him in the crowd as he struggled to hear.

When considering the entire spectrum of sympathy for Anabaptists ("half-Anabaptism"), it is quite possible that the Anabaptists and their sympathizers outnumbered (at least in some places) their determined Reformed opponents!

For the Reformed, half-Anabaptists were just as much a threat as the Anabaptists themselves. Half-Anabaptists, by their sympathy with dissenters, undermined the unity of the state church and brought into question its right and authority to enforce its understandings of doctrine.

To Verify a Rumor

It is never good to accept a rumor at face value. In fact, we need to be extremely suspicious of stories that come through several people, even well-meaning ones. Most likely, the stories coming to the Oberlanders about questionable teachings in the Emmental were from sources that they felt probably had some validity, because the churches decided to send a delegation to check things out. With the blessing and commission of the church, Jakob Ammann set out with fellow minister Niklaus Augsburger and others to find out if the stories were true.[16]

---

16   Here it is to be noted that the charge against Jakob Ammann that he was trying to push his

Off to Switzerland

When the investigation party arrived in Switzerland, they first went to Fridersmatt—about ten miles from Jakob's old stomping grounds in Oberhofen, as the crow flies—home of Niklaus Moser. Here Ammann asked Moser about the rumor that some of the Swiss ministers were comforting the Truehearted as being saved. Moser said he had heard no such thing.[17] Jakob then asked Moser what he believed about shunning and Moser said he agreed with Jakob.[18]

About this time, Hans Reist apparently had some problems in his congregation and asked Peter Giger and Niklaus Moser to help him. When Jakob heard of this, he asked Moser and Giger to do him a favor: Would they please ask Reist what his position on shunning was. The answer that came back was unsatisfactory to Jakob: "What goes into the mouth does not defile the person, but what comes out of the mouth, that defiles a man."[19] He further stated, "No sins pass in through the mouth."[20]

But Reist's answer seemed to charge the Oberlanders of thinking that the problem of eating with the excommunicated was in consuming food contaminated by a sinner. Had he thought through his response, it was he who missed the point: That which comes out defiles, indeed!

After receiving Reist's answer, Jakob told Niklaus Moser that

---

own will through, as some sort of dictator, is simply not true. It *may* be true that he had a large part in convincing the rest of the church and churches to send him, but that has no historical foundation. All through the painful division, Jakob never acted arbitrarily on his own, but always with others of his church. He was obviously a respected leader, but he was not a dictator operating without any oversight from others. Jakob Ammann, "Summary and Defense," in Roth, p. 39.

17   Christian Blank, "Summary and Defense," in Roth, p. 114.

18   Jakob Ammann, "Summary and Defense," in Roth, p. 30.

19   Peter Giger, "Summary and Defense," in Roth, p. 20.

20   Jakob Ammann, "Summary and Defense," in Roth, p. 28.

he wanted to go visit Reist himself. Moser suggested instead that they go see Bendicht Schneider, because he was the oldest leader.[21]

Instead, Jakob and his companions traveled to Rüttenen—35 miles north of Oberhofen—and decided to hold a preaching meeting near Peter Giger's home. Peter was already in bed, but when he received the invitation, he went to the meeting. After the meeting closed, Jakob and his companions—his brother Ulrich, Christian Blank, and Niklaus Augsburger—met in a side room with the Emmental ministers present: Michel of Blasen, Christian Gäumen, Peter Gäumen, Peter Giger, and others. Jakob and his companions presented their errand to the Swiss ministers, who were pleased. One of them even said that he had felt for some time that shunning should be investigated.[22] Peter Giger spoke in favor of shunning.[23]

While they were in the area, the investigation party summoned Niklaus Balzli and asked him if he thought the Truehearted were saved. He said he did not know anything about it and was not aware of having said so. He simply wanted to leave the issue to God's grace.[24]

So Far, So Good. But. . .

The investigation tour had gotten off to a good start. Hans Reist was the only one who had opposed them. From Rüttenen the party went to Uetigen. Jakob had Hans Reist show up there for a discussion about shunning, with both Ulli Ammann and Christian Blank being present as well. Jakob asked Hans if excommunicated individuals should be shunned in common ("physical") meals as well as communion ("spiritual meals"). Reist again refused to

---

21   Peter Giger, "Summary and Defense," in Roth, p. 20.

22   Ibid.

23   Christian Blank, "Summary and Defense," in Roth, p. 114.

24   Ibid., p. 114-115.

agree with this, replying that "No sins pass in through the mouth, because even Christ ate with tax collectors and sinners."[25]

Jakob then asked another question: Should obvious liars be excommunicated from the congregation? Reist replied in the negative. The investigators knew that Reist practiced what he preached on this point.[26] A woman in an Emmental Anabaptist congregation[27] had lied, then denied it when questioned. However, sufficient evidence existed which revealed her falsehood, and she finally admitted that she had lied. The case was twice brought before Hans Reist to be addressed, and both times he ruled that she should remain a sister in the congregation.[28]

Hans Reist was apparently disturbed by these unwelcome questionings throughout the Emmental congregations. He seems to have taken the investigative committee's inquisitiveness quite personally, as if Jakob and his friends were a direct threat to his authority. At the meeting, Reist—seemingly in an effort to silence or at least intimidate Ammann—made the astounding claim that he had more authority than Jakob! Jakob later wrote about this incident, pointing out, "but we are indeed in the same office. Is that not spiritual arrogance? Indeed, it seems as if he wishes to rule over the heritage of our faith in the assumption that one should follow the old ones even if their words and teaching do not conform to the word and teaching of God. . ."[29]

---

25   Jakob Ammann, "Summary and Defense," in Roth, p. 28.

26   Ibid.

27   This may have been in Reist's own congregation, but it is not known. It may have been referring to the story told above about the woman who claimed her husband was in town, when in fact he was in the cellar.

28   Ulli Ammann, "Summary and Defense," in Roth, p. 84.

29   Jakob Ammann, "Summary and Defense," in Roth, p. 29. Reist was only about five years older than Jakob, who was about 49 years old at the time, but Reist most likely had been in the ministry for a longer period of time than Jakob (since Jakob was a first-generation Anabaptist)—possibly many years longer.

The Truehearted—Ammann's balanced perspective

It is a common misunderstanding that Jakob Ammann taught that the Truehearted were not saved. Rather, he only taught that the Truehearted should not be told that they were saved. He acknowledged that they may indeed have made a true start in the Christian life, but should not be comforted as though they were safe where they were. Ammann also did not ask Anabaptists to shun the Truehearted. Ammann wrote:

> May it also be far from us that we want to judge or condemn anyone prematurely, for we know well that Scriptures says: Condemn not, so that you will not be condemned.
>
> There is One who will judge all people in His time, who will judge each according to his works, namely the Father who has given the judgment. We also do not know what kind of grace a sinner might attain before his death, therefore we have condemned no one.[1]

Ulli Ammann wrote:

> Since these people still adhere to worldly regulations and do what is commanded of them, even though they do give much help and charity to the pious which is indeed a very good means through God's mercy to find the right path. Nevertheless, these people are not to be regarded as saved because of their help and charity to the pious; but it is also good not to condemn them, but rather to praise them like the scripture says of Cornelius who also offered many prayers and alms, teaching well how Christianity should be begun.[2]

---

1   Jakob Ammann, "Summary and Defense," in Roth, p. 34.

2   Ulli Ammann, "Summary and Defense," in Roth, pp. 84-85.

Leaving Uetigen, Jakob and his companions went to Eggiwil and sent for Peter Habegger,[30] Peter Gerber from Golgraben, and Jakob Schwarz from Moos (near Langnau).[31] When asked about shunning, Habegger agreed with Jakob; Gerber and Schwarz could not agree on the spot, but they expressed a willingness to be convinced of the truth of shunning from God's Word.[32] They said that it would be best if a brotherhood council would decide the matter.[33]

Leaving Eggiwil, Jakob and his party returned to Fridersmatt—Moser's home—where Niklaus Augsburger was. In the meantime, Ammann sent two other ministers, Hans Gerber and Peter Zimmerman, to Hans Reist to ask him again if he would confess the shunning of the excommunicated. This time Hans simply refused to answer the question.[34]

Apparently unknown to the investigating party, Hans Reist had been quite busy after their meeting in Uetigen. He wrote a letter, with the approval of some other ministers and elders, saying that he refused to accept any command to shun the excommunicated in physical and spiritual meals. Furthermore, he stated that "one should not pay too much regard and attention to the younger [ministers] with respect to teaching and discipline."[35]

To say the least, Jakob was not pleased when he found out about

---

30   Called Peter Schwarzentruber by Jakob Ammann in "Summary and Defense," Roth, p. 30. He came from the Schwarzentrub farm near Trub (Hanspeter Jecker, personal communication).

31   Called Peter Golgraben by Christian Blank in "Summary and Defense," in Roth, p. 115. Golgraben is a place; the man's family name was Gerber (Hanspeter Jecker, personal communication).

32   Jakob Ammann, "Summary and Defense," in Roth, p. 30.

33   Christian Blank, "Summary and Defense," in Roth, p. 115.

34   Jakob Ammann, "Summary and Defense," in Roth, p. 28.

35   As reported by Jakob Ammann, "Summary and Defense," in Roth, pp. 28-29. Unfortunately, the full text of this letter has not been discovered.

this letter. With unfailing logic, he wrote later:

> Before this, however, neither Hans Reist nor anyone else ever issued
> a complaint that we did not use proper teaching and Christian
> discipline. If we were not following proper discipline and Christian
> teaching, why then did he not discipline us according to the church
> order and bring us around? If we, however, followed proper teach-
> ing and Christian discipline—as we hope has been the case—why
> then did he send a letter to the ministers and elders and warn them
> not to pay too much attention to the younger [ministers]?[36]

Back in Fridersmatt, Ammann concerned himself with the
problem of what to do about Hans Reist. Once more Jakob tried
to instruct him, sending Niklaus Augsburger and Hans Roller to
him.[37] This team of ministers asked Reist to stop comforting the
Truehearted with salvation, but he would not agree to this.[38]

What to do?

All of the Swiss ministers interviewed by Ammann and his
co-ministers had expressed themselves openly in favor of shunning
or at least not expressly opposed to it—except Reist. Jakob then
decided to get counsel from the Emmental ministers whom he had
been questioning in the previous days.[39] To this end, he called for
a ministers' meeting in Niklaus Moser's barn.[40] Hans Reist was
invited.[41]

---

36   Jakob Ammann, "Summary and Defense," in Roth, p. 29.

37   Jakob may have gone with them, but that is not clear.

38   Jakob Ammann, "Summary and Defense," in Roth, p. 30.

39   Ibid., pp. 30-31.

40   Peter Giger, "Summary and Defense," in Roth, p. 21.

41   Christian Blank, "Summary and Defense," in Roth, p. 115.

The Truehearted—A Reformed view

Jakob Ammann was concerned that consoling the Truehearted
with salvation could lead to them being comfortable in their lack
of commitment and surrender to the cross. George Thormann, a
Reformed pastor pleading with people not to leave the state church,
took exactly this view from the Anabaptists' own words. Writing to
Reformed people who were attracted to the Anabaptists, he argued
that since the Anabaptists themselves acknowledge that one could
be saved in the state church, it was therefore wholly unnecessary to
leave the state church and join the Anabaptists.

The day of the meeting came, but Hans Reist did not.[42] In fact,
only a few Emmental ministers showed up—Niklaus Moser, Peter
Giger, Peter Habegger (Schwartzentruber), and Peter Gerber.[43] All
of them—with the possible exception of Peter Gerber—had earlier
expressed support for Ammann's view of shunning.[44] Now they
found themselves in a very awkward predicament. They had earlier
given their word to Jakob Ammann that they supported shunning;
furthermore, some of the Emmental ministers had stated that there
were plenty of Scriptures in favor of shunning and had even practiced shunning previously in their own congregations.[45] But now,
Hans Reist had expressed displeasure at his would-be instructors
and had definitively opposed shunning. What were they to do?
Abide by their confession to the Oberlanders and fall under the
displeasure of Hans Reist? Or, side with Reist and try to convince

42   Ibid..

43   Peter Giger, "Summary and Defense," in Roth, p. 21. Giger called Gerber "Peter of
Goul."

44   Jakob Ammann, "Summary and Defense," in Roth, p. 30.

45   Ulli Ammann, "Summary and Defense," in Roth, p. 84.

Ammann to not be so radical? The investigation, which had begun
so well, was now in a quandary; the Emmental ministers were
being forced to take sides.

When Jakob Ammann arrived at the Moser barn with Niklaus
Augsburger and Christian Blank, it did not take him long to notice—probably with some alarm—that the Emmentalers were
wavering in their commitment. Could it be possible that his supporters would turn out to be fair-weather friends?

The Emmentaler ministers present now showed a reluctance to
discuss the issue of shunning, and even argued against it. Jakob
said their reasonings were "with Scripture but without sound arguments."[46] Obviously, this was Jakob's point of view. The other
side probably felt otherwise.

Turning Back

Jakob then asked Niklaus Moser what he personally believed
about shunning. Remember, not long before, Moser had said he
agreed with Jakob. Moser replied that "it would be better to wait
for what a common council might decide in the matter." Ammann
replied that Moser "was a minister and should teach his faith to
the laity."[47] Here a matter in church polity was exposed. The Swiss
Brethren had taken a more congregational approach to church
organization, meaning that the final "authority" in deciding what
was correct doctrine and practice lay in the whole congregation,
not in the ministry by itself. The Dutch Anabaptists seemed to
have taken a more ministry-led approach.

Jakob then questioned Peter Giger what his personal view of
shunning was. He replied that he "would give no other counsel

46   Jakob Ammann, "Summary and Defense," in Roth, pp. 30-31.

47   Christian Blank, "Summary and Defense," in Roth, p. 115.

That which comes out defiles

Do the Scriptures quoted by the Emmentaler ministers about that which comes out of the mouth, not what goes in, have anything to do with shunning? The reason for shunning is not because an unrepentant sinner defiles the physical food, but because he will likely open his mouth and spew out the uncleanness of his heart. The carnal young girl, for example, who loved pretty dresses and flirting with the young men and refused to repent and thus had to be put away from the flock will very likely try to convince other young girls to join her in her folly. Yes, that which comes out of the mouth defiles, and that is one of the reasons the carnal are to be avoided: They may try to convince others to follow them.

than that the elders and ministers in Switzerland come together, search the word of God and test the gospel, and whichever is closest to the gospel, that will be my decision."[48] The other Emmental ministers expressed agreement with Moser and Giger.

Thus the Emmental ministers turned back from supporting the Oberlanders. While not totally rejecting the idea of shunning, they pushed the decision onto the shoulders of a future church council. This put Jakob Ammann on the spot. He had good reasons for wanting to finish his mission and return to his home in tolerant Alsace. An ongoing threat of arrest was continually hanging over his head. On June 28, 1693, an arrest warrant had been issued for "the Anabaptist preachers altogether, but also the preacher Amman in particular." A *Täuferjäger*[49] by the name of Peter Erb had been given the special task of arresting the "chief Anabaptist

---

48   Peter Giger, "Summary and Defense," in Roth, p. 21.

49   Anabaptist hunter.

Would you travel to hear Ammann preach?

Investigating church problems was not the only thing Jakob Ammann did on this trip to Switzerland. He also seems to have preached at more than one meeting. Several months later, a non-Anabaptist named Christian Schönauer was accused of "running about here and there, in various households, to hear the preaching of the cursed Jaggi Amman."[1]

---

1   Leroy Beachy, *Unser Leit: The Story of the Amish*, 2011, Goodly Heritage Books, Volume 1, p. 68.

Jaggi Amman."[50]

This threat of arrest may have been the motivation to hurry up the next meeting. Jakob suggested it be in eight days. Peter Giger suggested three weeks, but Ammann said that was too long. Niklaus Moser then suggested fourteen days, to which everyone agreed.[51] Jakob mentioned that "a special effort" should be made to have Hans Reist present at the meeting.[52]

The Emmentaler ministers immediately sent out messengers to invite the other ministers to the second meeting. On the appointed day, many of the Emmentaler ministers and lay brothers and sisters gathered[53]—probably again in Moser's barn. Niklaus Moser, Peter Giger, Peter Gerber, Jakob Schwartz, Peter Habegger (Schwarzentruber), and Hans Müller were present, in addition to

---

50   Leroy Beachy, *Unser Leit: The Story of the Amish*, 2011, Goodly Heritage Books, Volume 1, p. 75.

51   Peter Giger, "Summary and Defense," in Roth, p. 21.

52   Leroy Beachy, *Unser Leit: The Story of the Amish*, 2011, Goodly Heritage Books, Volume 1, p. 77; Christian Blank, "Summary and Defense," in Roth, p. 116.

53   Christian Blank, "Summary and Defense," in Roth, p. 116.

The Froschauer Bible

When the Swiss Anabaptists quote Scripture, it does not always match exactly what our present-day English or German Bibles say. This is because the Bible they were most familiar with was the Swiss Froschauer Bible, which has some slight differences from the King James and Luther Bibles.

Based in part on Luther's German translation work, the Froschauer Bible was produced by Reformers in Switzerland and printed by Christoph Froschauer in Zürich. The New Testament was printed in 1524; by 1529, the entire Bible had been published by Froschauer in Swiss German.

The Froschauer translation, naturally enough, was the most-used Bible among Swiss Anabaptists. When Protestant scholars corrected errors in the earlier printings and published revised Froschauer Bibles, the Anabaptists were highly skeptical of the revisions and continued using the older editions. When they became scarce, the Anabaptists reprinted the New Testament several times. (Once they reprinted the entire Bible). Angered, the Bernese government outlawed the reprints, which became known as *Täufertestaments* (Anabaptist Testaments).

In America, many Swiss Anabaptists continued to use the Froschauer Bible, but Luther's German translation was much more accessible in colonial America. The German Baptist printer Christopher Sauer printed the first German Bible in America—Luther's—in 1743. Luther's translation eventually displaced Froschauer's among American Anabaptists, although ministers continued to use and quote from it for many decades. Today, the Hutterites still use the Froschauer Bible.

Hans Reist

We know very little about the life of Hans Reist—even less than we know about Jakob Ammann. In 1670, his house was confiscated by the Bernese government and he and his wife, Barbara Ryser, were banished from the Canton of Bern, penniless. His house was in Rotenbaum, in a small valley which had so many Anabaptists that it was nicknamed "Anabaptist Vale." Hans and his wife lived in the Palatinate for some time.

By the 1680s, Reist was back in the Emmental. He appears to have been one of the main Anabaptist bishops in the area during the Amish dispute. In 1701, he was arrested and he promised to attend state church services and accept the state church sacraments. Whether he kept this promise—or whether he ever intended to—is unknown.

others.[54, 55] Jakob Ammann and nine of the ministers from his side showed up.[56]

No-Show Reist

The group waited for Hans Reist. Jakob and the Oberlander ministers "spoke to them in all kindness and love and said if they could correct us using God's Word, then we wanted to be directed and instructed by them," as Jakob later remembered.[57] Peter Giger took Jakob up on this offer and began quoting Scriptures: "What goes into the mouth does not defile a man, but that which comes

---

54   Peter Giger, "Summary and Defense," in Roth, p. 21; Leroy Beachy, *Unser Leit: The Story of the Amish*, 2011, Goodly Heritage Books, Volume 1, p. 77.

55   Jakob Ammann, "Summary and Defense," in Roth, p. 31.

56   Peter Giger, "Summary and Defense," in Roth, p. 21.

57   Jakob Ammann, "Summary and Defense," in Roth, p. 31.

out of the mouth defiles a man" (Matthew 15:11).

Here was the same old nonsense that Hans Reist had thrown at them before. Jakob replied that the verse did not apply to the situation, "waving his hand." Giger then quoted Romans 14:3: "He who eats does not judge another who eats."

Jakob waved his hand, likely with growing frustration by the minute, and replied that "it had nothing to do with the matter."

Next Giger quoted Galatians 5:15: "When you are biting and devouring among yourselves, watch out that you do not end up consuming each other." He then added, "Therefore, take heed dear brothers."

The Emmentalers then pled with Jakob that "for God's sake. . . he should not create more confusion or a division, or cause such anguish and confusion."[58] They were likely in distress over their predicament; being caught in the middle of the disagreement between Reist and Ammann was just no fun. Reist's absence was not helping the situation either. Jakob replied: "We will not always travel about; I will not cause a division."[59] Obviously, tensions were mounting on both sides.

But it is Harvest Time!

Finally, the ministers decided to find out what was keeping Hans Reist away. Three sisters were present, and one of them was sent to find out why Reist was not there yet.[60] Shortly a message arrived: "They could not come [since] it was in the middle of harvest

---

58   Peter Giger, "Summary and Defense," in Roth, pp. 21-22.

59   Ibid., p. 22.

60   Ibid. It is possible that it was some laymen *(geschwistert)* rather than sisters *(schwestern)* who were sent—see Leroy Beachy, *Unser Leit: The Story of the Amish*, 2011, Goodly Heritage Books, Volume 1, p. 78.

Your clothes are too worldly!

One myth about the Amish division is that it had something to do with clothing. There is little evidence that clothing had much to do with the division. Jakob Ammann made only one vague comment about dress and grooming:

> I have also excommunicated no one . . . on questions of clothing or styling beards, or long hair. . . If there would be someone who wants to be conformed to the world with shaved beard, with long hair, and haughty clothing and does not acknowledge that it is wrong, he should in all fairness be punished. For God has no pleasure in the proud.[1]

The fact that Jakob mentioned the issue perhaps indicates that there was some discussion about it; however, this is the only mention of clothing and grooming from the participants in the division.

In 1697, Dutch/North German Mennonite minister Gerritt Roosen wrote a letter to the Swiss Brethren in Alsace, weighing in on the division. He apparently understood the division to be mostly about clothing, and had probably been misinformed.

---

1   Jakob Ammann, "Summary and Defense," in Roth, p. 40.

---

and a busy time."[61] Of course, Reist did not directly say that *he* was busy harvesting; he only said it was harvest time. What was Reist's real motivation for not coming?

Reist's apparent lack of concern for meeting to discuss matters concerning the church—for the second time—was too much for Jakob Ammann. It was very obvious that he simply did not want

---

61   Peter Giger, "Summary and Defense," in Roth, p. 22.

to come. This was the straw that broke the camel's back. Greatly irritated,[62] Jakob said "This is the way they act, that they indeed cannot be persuaded to come here. . . Hans Reist [is] a rabble-rouser who slandered and shamed God's Word."[63]

It appears that Jakob probably expected that Reist was not ready to agree with him, for he pulled a ready-made letter out of his pocket containing six charges against Hans Reist.[64] After all six charges had been read, Ammann said that Reist "should be excommunicated and banned from the Christian church and the fellowship of God."

Horror in the House of God

The Emmentaler ministers were horrified that the excommunication did not follow their procedure,[65] which would have included receiving counsel from the entire congregation before excommunicating someone. However, in Jakob's mind, Reist had already received four admonitions—much more than the two required by Scripture (Titus 3:10-11).[66]

But worse horror was yet to come! Jakob then asked Moser and Giger "if they intended to affirm him in this." Niklaus Moser replied, "Show as much forbearance as possible for I have as heavy a burden as you. I have not yet asked or consulted with the lay brothers and sisters. I cannot promise for the others." Jakob replied, "You should have already consulted and asked them."

---

62   Christian Blank, "Summary and Defense," in Roth, p. 116. Roth translates *"fast verdriezlich"* in Blank's letter as "almost became enraged," but Beachy (*Unser Leit: The Story of the Amish*, 2011, Goodly Heritage Books, Volume 1, p. 79) argues that it should be translated "became extremely annoyed."

63   Peter Giger, "Summary and Defense," in Roth, p. 22.

64   Unfortunately, the text of this letter has not been discovered.

65   Peter Giger, "Summary and Defense," in Roth, p. 22.

66   Jakob Ammann, "Summary and Defense," in Roth, pp. 8-30.

The Dortrecht Confession

Many accounts of the Amish division emphasize the role played by the Dortrecht Confession. Dortrecht, like the Amish, taught the shunning of the excommunicated, and also taught footwashing (practiced by the Amish and a point of contention between the two sides later in the division).

The Dortrecht Confession may indeed have influenced the Amish side; however, to imagine that it took center stage in the debates, or that either side was consciously trying to follow (or not follow) it, is probably going beyond what the evidence shows.

Jakob Ammann only mentioned the Dortrecht Confession once, and he comes across as looking down on those who must "look to the old" as opposed to himself, who only needed the Word of God.

If you are able to correct us from God's Word, however, then we want to allow ourselves to be instructed and you will have won the case. But we say it once again: It must be proven from God's Word, for we pay no regard to human councils, to longstanding practice and the custom of time if they are not established according to God's Word. For our faith should be loudly, clearly, firmly, and solely grounded upon God's word. This is the proper council which the Father and the Son and the Holy Spirit have decided together in their wise council chambers and [which] the only begotten Son of God has sealed with His rose-colored and precious blood. We should be looking to this. If you, however, want to look to the old, then look to the confession of faith established in Holland, made in the city of Dordrecht, which conforms to the Word of God.[1]

Ulrich Ammann mentions the Dortrecht Confession more fa-
vorably. He says it was "approved from there [Holland] clear to
Switzerland as scripturally correct and good and was a common
confession of our faith among all of us in Switzerland," and also
points out that it had been given to the Bernese government as the
Swiss Brethren's confession of faith. Ulrich also said that "numerous
confessions of faith and true histories" teach the Amish views on
the disputed matters.[2]

Two Reistian authors also tried to prove that the Dortrecht
Confession supported their views on excommunication.

The Dortrecht Confession was certainly part of the story of the
Amish division; however, it seems that it was not the focal point of
controversy.

1   Jakob Ammann, "Summary and Defense," in Roth, p. 39.

2   Ulli Ammann, "Summary and Defense," in Roth, pp. 93, 98.

Jakob then asked Peter Giger again "if he intended to affirm it
with him." Giger replied, "I will not at this time give you a decision
other than what I have already stated. I can give no other counsel
than that the elders meet, and they are simply not all here."[67]

Perhaps Peter Giger had forgotten that he had previously said
that he agreed with social shunning, but Jakob Ammann did not
forget. To Jakob, going back on one's word like this was nothing
less than lying, which could not be tolerated in the church.[68] Thus

to Moser and Giger, Jakob said, "Then you should be excommunicated and banned as liars."

Jakob then asked Peter Gerber, Peter Habegger, and Jakob Schwarz "if they would confess shunning with him." They likewise refused to confess it. Jakob excommunicated them.[69]

He then turned to Hans Müller, a minister from the Aargau, for his opinion on shunning. He refused to confess it. This time, Jakob did not give an excommunication, because this was the first time Hans had been questioned.[70] The Oberlander investigative committee was extremely scrupulous about carrying out the correct scriptural procedures for excommunication, in this case giving at least two admonitions for heresy (Titus 3:10-11).

Ammann also excommunicated Niklaus Balzli, with no admonitions, for lying.[71] Since this was a different category of sin, the Oberlanders felt that it could be dealt with immediately rather than giving at least two admonitions.

The Aftershock

Having excommunicated Hans Reist and six other ministers,[72] the Oberlanders had probably greatly shocked the lay members present. Many of them begged him to show forbearance; one sister fell on her knees before Jakob and begged him to show forbearance.[73] But Jakob was not to be moved. He had shown much patience already for weeks, something the lay members may not have realized. The excommunications were not a totally rash,

69   Peter Giger, "Summary and Defense," in Roth, pp. 22-23.

70   Jakob Ammann, "Summary and Defense," in Roth, p. 31.

71   The sources do not indicate what the lie was. Jakob Ammann, "Summary and Defense," in Roth, p. 32.

72   Christian Blank, "Summary and Defense," in Roth, p. 116.

73   Ibid.

Am I understanding you correctly?

When considering the Amish dispute, it is good to keep in mind that while the various letters give fairly consistent accounts of the meetings that were held and what happened, the details of the issues at stake are mostly represented in letters written by the Amish side. Only two Emmentalers—Niklaus Moser and Peter Giger—wrote letters describing their side of the story, and neither is long on doctrinal details. If Jakob Ammann and his side had somehow misunderstood the other side in some way, it would be almost impossible for us to know without further letters.

We know that more letters were written during the dispute. Letters which have survived mention or quote from other letters which do not survive. We can guess that there were probably many more which disappeared from the historical record completely. Most puzzling is that while Hans Reist wrote at least one letter during the dispute, it was apparently not preserved, nor any other writings from him regarding the division.

one-question action by a dictator who wanted to control everyone else. Jakob's companion, Peter Zimmerman, announced, "There you have it."[74] Then Ammann and his ministers left the barn without shaking hands with anyone—not even those who had not been excommunicated.

About noon on the same day, seven more ministers—seemingly from Ammann's side—showed up and called another meeting in the area, but forbade that the excommunicants be told of it. Apparently the Reistians did not expect Ammann to actually

---

74   What he exactly meant by that statement is not known, but it seemed to indicate a finality to the matter.

Questions to ponder

The story of the Amish division and how the conflict escalated brings many questions to mind.

- How similar do different congregations in a church group or conference need to be? Ammann insisted on united practice across congregations, whereas the Emmentalers were willing to tolerate some differences.

- How should unacceptable differences be dealt with?

- Which differences are worth dividing a church group over?

- Is provocative and uncooperative behavior like Hans Reist's acceptable when the church is trying to work through issues?

- How can we maintain calmness and peace when the stress of the situation builds, tempting us to rash words and actions we may later regret?

- Is the way we relate to issues sometimes more important than which side we take on the issue itself?

practice what he preached about shunning, for Peter Giger was offended at not having been invited and later complained, "Consider carefully, is that according to love?"[75]

Afterwards, many of the Emmental brothers met to discuss whether Ammann's excommunications should be honored or not. They decided that Moser and Giger should, for a time at least, cease all ministerial duties. Then they counseled privately some more, called Moser and Giger to them, and reinstated them to their ministerial positions.[76]

---

75   Peter Giger, "Summary and Defense," in Roth, p. 23.

76   Ibid.

Not too long afterward, the Oberlanders sent Hans Gerber and Christian Blank to Hans Müller and Bendicht Schneider. They went to the older minister Schneider and asked him if he had been questioned about shunning. He replied that he had been questioned twice. The investigators asked him one more time whether he would confess shunning. He refused to do so and even vehemently argued against it. He also refused to confess that open sinners should be excommunicated. Nevertheless, Schneider gave his questioners a bit of solid advice: "One should not excommunicate unless the entire congregation was agreed on it."[77]

At that point in his life, Jakob scoffed at that idea, commenting "as if the keys [of the Kingdom] had been given to all the members of the congregation."[78] But Jakob would later regret having performed excommunications without the counsel of the congregation.

Gerber and Blank then asked Hans Müller if he would accept shunning, but he did not want to. Returning to Jakob Ammann, the two investigators informed him of the results of their interviews. On hearing the news, Ammann and his fellow-ministers produced the following document and sent it to the Emmentalers.

> I, Jakob Ammann, together with twelve ministers and elders. It is our will and intention, and this in accordance with the Word of God, that because Bendicht Schneider and Hans of Wiler [Hans Müller] do not wish to confess the faith with us, they should be excommunicated and banned from the Christian church and godly fellowship as heretical persons.[79]

---

77   Jakob Ammann, "Summary and Defense," in Roth, p. 31.

78   Ibid., pp. 31-32.

79   As recorded by Peter Giger, "Summary and Defense," in Roth, p. 23.

Are You Sure?

In response to these latest excommunications, the Emmentalers wrote Jakob Ammann and his companions a note which asked them "whether they wished to acknowledge that they had gone too far with rebuking and banning, and this for the third time."[80] The Oberlanders replied, "If you do not wish to confess shunning, then we do not want to have anything to do with you."[81] To the Oberlanders at this time, the only thing that could bring about a reconciliation was repentance. Later, they would humble themselves and acknowledge that they had moved too fast.

After a messenger to the Oberlanders was not received, Peter Giger and Hans Zaugg went themselves to visit the Ammann brothers. They begged Jakob and Ulli to call another meeting to which the lay brothers and sisters would be permitted to come. Jakob replied that he "did not want to start any new discussion"[82] with the Emmentalers. Peter Giger begged Jakob three times "for the sake of God," but Jakob was adamant.[83] However, after the two men had left, Jakob changed his mind and sent a note saying that he wanted to come after all.

Jakob and his fellow ministers came, but without any lay members with them. Perhaps they thought it would have been rather foolhardy to expose a large group to danger traveling across a canton which was actively hunting for Anabaptists.

At the beginning of the meeting, a rule was agreed upon: "When someone is speaking, the other should listen."[84] Jakob spoke while

---

80   Ibid. It is unclear whether they wrote three notes or thought Ammann went too far three times.

81   Ibid., pp. 23-24.

82   Ibid., p. 24.

83   Ibid.

84   Ibid.

the rest listened. Then Peter Giger stood up to speak—and Jakob stood up to leave! Peter grabbed Jakob by the sleeve and said, "Let me also finish my speech."[85] Jakob pulled his arm away and left.

We do not know what Jakob's reason for this disrespectful action was. He might have thought that since Giger was excommunicated, he had no right to address an assembly of the saints. However, from the other side's point of view, this seems to have appeared to be simple arrogance.

Summary

This confrontation during the summer of 1693 was only the beginning of a painful division. At the conclusion of the confrontation, nine Emmental Anabaptist ministers had been excommunicated by the Oberlanders. There were obvious deficiencies in the Emmentaler churches, which the Oberlanders tried to address, but they sometimes failed in their attitudes.

We must remember that, as far as we know, all the Oberlander ministers were first-generation Anabaptists. As such, their methods of dealing with sin in the church did not have the years of experience that we may take for granted. Jakob had been an Anabaptist less than fifteen years, and his brother Ulli for perhaps only half that amount. Within a decade, the Oberlanders would express extreme repentance for the *way*[86] they had handled the matter.

Jakob Ammann's actions were not always above reproach. Yet we should recognize that he probably truly meant well; he believed that sin was in the camp. He was under extreme pressure, both from the state that was hunting his head and from fellow ministers who one day said they supported him and only days later suddenly

---

85　Ibid.

86　Not the issues, but the manner in which they handled it.

Good or evil?

The Bible says "let not then your good be evil spoken of" (Romans 14:16). Jakob may have meant well by leaving the meeting when Peter Giger began to speak, but when one agrees to a meeting that aims for reconciliation, giving your side of the story and then walking off will hardly be taken as a spirit of humility and teachableness. The following piece of poetry says it well:

For me t'was not the truth you taught,

To you so clear, to me so dim,

But when you came to me,

You brought a deeper sense of Him.

And from your eyes He beckoned me,

And from your heart, His love was shed.

'Til I lost sight of you,

And saw the Christ instead.

—Unknown

said they did not. Unfortunately, it seems for the next 250 years, many would not forgive Jakob Ammann for his failures in the matter—even though, as we shall see, he later humbled himself and admitted he had erred.

The Oberlanders probably started out with all good intentions and attitudes, yet the pressure of the situation got the best of them in some instances. This created unnecessary pain and distrust in some who otherwise may have eventually acknowledged the sin in their midst.

As it was, it seems evident that the whole underlying source of stress was that of friction between an older, lukewarm, "established" Anabaptism with a newer, zealous, and revived group of fresh converts. This same story has been repeated again and again throughout church history (and had happened many times before this occasion, as well). The new converts want purity and consistency, while those who have grown up in the movement do not like the boat getting rocked.

The zeal of the new Oberlander converts and the laxity of at least some of the lukewarm "established" Emmentalers would very likely have clashed sooner or later even if Jakob Ammann would never have been involved. It is time that Jakob quits getting blamed for the division. Yes, his failures added fuel to the fire, but underlying the whole situation were two visions, two irreconcilable visions: church discipline and permissiveness, zeal and lukewarmness.

If. . . it is considered necessary to speak of it [the division] for the furtherance of God's honor and human well-being, then one should go freely down the straight path with the spirit of truth and discuss the entire background without any partiality, not to present something as uncharitably as possible in order to insult or belittle one's fellow human being and to hide something else to protect oneself. For without any question, mistakes were made on both sides and therefore each person should carry his own burden and it is proper for each person to reconcile himself again with God and with the aggrieved fellow human whom he has wronged.

—Ulli Ammann, 1698

Roth, p. 83

CHAPTER 7

The Rift Deepens

s the schism came to reality in the Emmental, both sides attempted to get the ministers in the Palatinate (southwestern Germany) to side with them. The Emmentalers wrote an account of the confrontation, complaining of Jakob's "harsh actions."[1] The Alsatians, normally affiliated with Jakob, wrote a letter (apparently with Jakob's knowledge) to the Palatines asking for help with the issues of the division.[2] Jakob himself also wrote to the Palatines, trying to convince them of the truth of shunning.[3]

The majority of Palatine ministers apparently took the side of the Emmentalers. They wrote one or possibly two letters to Ammann and the Alsatian ministers. The text of their letter(s) has not been found, but from other letters we learn that the Palatine ministers

---

1   Christian Blank, "Summary and Defense," in Roth, p. 116.

2   Part of this letter is copied in Jonas Lohr, "Jonas Lohr to Jakob Ammann," in Roth, pp. 59-60. Jakob Ammann may have been referring to this letter on p. 43 of Roth.

3   Jakob Ammann, "Summary and Defense," in Roth, p. 43. Unfortunately, this letter has not been discovered.

never directly responded to what Jakob wrote,[4] but instead asked the Alsatians why they had allowed one man (Jakob Ammann) to turn them from their old church order to a "new one," and commanding them to not observe shunning.[5] They also begged the "Amish" and the Reistians to be reconciled with each other and to abstain from dividing the church.[6]

Meanwhile, the Emmentaler ministers were quite busy. The "Amish" were not yet finished with their investigation; there were congregations and ministers whom they had not yet visited or questioned. The Emmentalers made an active effort to enlist these "neutral" congregations for their side. Ulli Ammann later wrote:

> They sent out messengers to the brothers and sisters day and night and also went out themselves and denounced us saying we had proceeded so roughly with them and had put them under an unjust ban. If we came and wanted to visit them, [they wrote,] then they should not receive us at all. They reported to many brothers and sisters their side of the dispatched articles which made them afraid and pulled their hearts away from us. Then when we came and wanted to speak with these people, they hid themselves from us, those who earlier had been well-disposed to us.
>
> Thus, the hearts of many people were separated and distanced from us and became a source of the division.[7]

To be sure, both sides obviously wanted the congregations who had not been involved thus far to hear their side of the story, and most likely they wanted their side to be heard first. It appears that

---

4   Ibid. Jakob wrote: "We would appreciate a response to this letter."

5   Ibid., pp. 39, 41, 44.

6   Christian Blank, "Summary and Defense," in Roth, p. 116.

7   Ulli Ammann, "Summary and Defense," in Roth, p. 86.

Jakob's father

Five years before the confrontations in the Emmental, in May 1688, Jakob's parents had been summoned before the authorities of Erlenbach on suspicion of being Anabaptists. They denied the charge, but now, after having moved to Steffisburg, the aged Michel Ammann and his daughter, Cathrina, were summoned again before the Erlenbach authorities in July 1693. They were questioned because they had been skipping Reformed worship and communion. This time, they did not deny being Anabaptists. The authorities told the Ammanns that they would be considered Anabaptists and punished if they did not attend communion in the fall.

This would have been at the same time that the Oberlanders were dealing with the Emmentalers. So while Jakob had church issues he was trying to work through, he also had some family issues to deal with, namely his almost 80-year-old father needing to hide from coming persecution for embracing Anabaptism. Michel soon ended up in the Alsace, quite possibly with Jakob's help.

the Emmentalers had a head start in some situations, which upset the Oberlanders. Ulli Ammann felt that this closed the door so much that they could not even present their side of the story, much less present it first.

These circumstances were apparently the motivation[8] for the Oberlanders to write a "Warning Letter":

I, Jakob Ammann, together with the ministers and elders, send this writing and wish to make it known to everyone, be they women or men, ministers or disciples in the church, to everyone in the

8   Ibid.

Arrest order for Jakob Ammann

We have considered it needful [concerning] Jaggi Amman, an arch-Anabaptist who roves here and there in the country, to allow earnest inquiry in so far, that the person who discovers him and hands him over, may expect a hundred Thalers from us.[1]

---

1   Hanspeter Jecker, "Jakob Ammanns missglückte Verhaftung im Bernbiet 1694," *Mennonitica Helvetica* 18 (1995); translated by John B. Martin.

general, that you—namely those who, after counsel and judgment, were not excommunicated from the church—should appear and report to us on the 20th of February, and you should give an account as to whether you can confess the disputed articles with us. . . Or, if you can teach otherwise from God's Word we want to allow ourselves to be taught. If, however, you do not want to appear on this specified day to confess these articles with us or to show us otherwise on the basis of God's Word, then we want to set another specified time—namely, on the 7th day of March—for you to account for yourselves. If, however, you do not appear at this appointed time and date to account for yourselves, then you. . . shall be excommunicated from the fellowship of God beginning with us, the ministers and elders, and especially by me, Jakob Ammann, as sectarians, and you shall be shunned and avoided until the time of your repentance according to God's Word.[9]

Ulli Ammann later wrote that they chose this method because

---

9   Jakob Ammann et al., "Letter of Warning," in Roth, pp. 25-26.

"we at that time did not know a better way."[10]

In the meantime, Jakob may have slipped quietly out of Switzerland and back home—probably with his aged father and perhaps his sister.[11] Michael Ammann settled in the Catholic village of Heidolsheim, where he seems to have openly joined an Anabaptist congregation.

Arch-heretic

If Jakob had left Bern, the government of Bern apparently did not know it. On December 14, 1693, Bern made an order and sent it to seven districts, instructing officials to watch for "Jaggi Amman of Oberhofen, a roving arch-Anabaptist." A reward of 100 Thalers was offered for his arrest.[12]

While the Bern authorities may not have heard of Jakob's departure, the Reformed church *had* heard of the controversy among the Anabaptists. Johann Rudolf Salchli was a Reformed pastor in Eggiwil, an area with many Anabaptists. Salchli was a committed opponent of Anabaptism. Having read Georg Thormann's book *Probier-Stein*, Salchli wrote Thormann a letter regarding Anabaptism. In the letter he mentioned Jakob Ammann and his travels through the canton. Salchli understood Ammann to be teaching that the Reformed could not be saved, and that Reformed communion was the "table of devils." (This was probably based on Ammann's teaching about the Truehearted.) Regarding the division and dispute among the Anabaptists, Salchli repeated gossip he had heard, that the Anabaptists had completely given themselves

---

10   Ulli Ammann, "Summary and Defense," in Roth, p. 86.

11   On the other hand, he may have stayed in Switzerland longer, as suggested by Hanspeter Jecker, "Jakob Ammanns missglückte Verhaftung im Bernbiet 1694," *Mennonitica Helvetica* 18 (1995).

12   John Hüppi, "Identifying Jacob Ammann," *Mennonite Quarterly Review* 74(2) (April 2000):329-339, p. 329.

to "the deceiver Ammann," submitting to his "yoke" which was so burdensome that the Anabaptists were afraid, and many who had thought of converting were deterred from doing so. While Salchli's perception of the situation was inaccurate, it seems entirely credible that the fellowship-shattering dispute may indeed have deterred some interested people from joining the Anabaptists.[13]

In the fall, after the Oberlanders had excommunicated the Emmentaler ministers, Jakob began to write his "Long Letter."[14] He wrote in response to the letter(s) of the Palatine ministers who had written to Ammann and the Alsatians. He began:

> Along with a very friendly greeting, we wish you bodily health and the salvation of your souls from our whole hearts, especially I, Jakob Ammann, together with my co-workers in the house of God, ministers and elders in Switzerland, to you the ministers and elders in the Upper and Lower Palatinate. Think well of us in your prayers. We are also minded to pray [on your behalf] inasmuch as the Lord grants His grace. Amen.[15]

Jakob went on to describe the events of the confrontation and division up to that point, and to define and defend his point of view regarding the issues of the division. He wrote with clarity and passion. Toward the end of the letter, however, he began to directly scold the Palatine ministers: "You ignorant Galatians! Consider who has bewitched you so that you do not believe the truth."[16] He wrote:

---

13   Hanspeter Jecker (with Heinrich Löffler), "'Wie dem schädlichen Übel der Taüfferey zu remedieren sey' - Zwei Briefe des Pfarrers Johann Rudolf Salchli von Eggiwil im Emmental (1693f.)," *Mennonitica Helvetica* 28/29 (2005/2006):89-145.

14   Called the "Summary and Defense" in Roth, pp. 27-45. It was dated November 22, 1693.

15   Jakob Ammann, "Summary and Defense," in Roth, p. 27.

16   Ibid., p. 42.

Note well the matter which was concocted and spoken of in Alsace and Markirch in which you asked them not to comply too rigorously [with us], neither to use or to maintain shunning. You asked of us, however, that we should again make compromises with these liars, apostates, heretical people and rabble-rousers and to surrender ourselves to them: people who have already been banned by the Word of God and who should be separated and shunned until the time of their repentance according to the Word of God.[17]

Jakob's statement that the Reistians were "liars, apostates, heretical people and rabble-rousers" was quite offensive to the Reistians. However, in justice to Jakob, when he wrote this, he was not simply pulling a string of negative adjectives from the lexicon and attaching them to his opponents. There was a specific reason why each and every word was chosen exactly as Jakob wrote it. Later, Ulli Ammann (who had signed Jakob's "Long Letter") explained:

We also believed and confessed that in our talk and writing we did not act appropriately when we rebuked them as liars, quarrelers, apostates, and rabble-rousers even though we were given sufficient reason and cause by them for such names. Those who confessed the required articles with us at the beginning gave us cause to call them liars. . . . Later, when these men saw that Hans Reist, and others as well, did not want to confess the stated articles with us, they also retreated from their confession and opposed [us] like the others.[18]

In other words, they called those who had abruptly changed their mind "liars" for one day agreeing with them, and then suddenly

---

17   Ibid., p. 42.

18   Ulli Ammann, "Summary and Defense," in Roth, pp. 92-93.

Grounded Upon God's Word

not agreeing. "Quarrelers" is a fairly obvious accusation, but one that could have applied to both sides. "Apostates" is another obvious word that they felt truly applied to the situation; one day agreeing with what the Oberlanders saw as the true faith, a few days later, not. "Rabble-rousers" (ones who stir up other people) or "trouble-makers" was applied to them because rather than humbly accepting the church discipline that was applied to them, the excommunicated ones wrote letters and tried to stir up others against the ones administering the discipline.

What a mess! The Oberlanders meant well in trying to deal with sin in the camp, but did not recognize until later that they were adding sin (in the form of their wrong attitudes) to the situation. How they later regretted using some of those adjectives!

Underhanded Church Politics

The Ohnenheim Conference was an example of terrible, underhanded church politics.

After issuing the "Warning Letter," the Oberlanders probably anxiously awaited a delegation from at least *some* of the other Swiss Brethren churches—but apparently no one showed up. Jakob and his fellow-ministers then "judged [them to be] apart from the church" for failing to appear at the stated times and because they "wanted to adhere to the men who had been disciplined."[19]

Some of the Palatine ministers, however, had an admirable desire for peace—and they were willing to put in the time, effort, and money necessary to help the two sides become reconciled with each other. They were not content to simply ask the sides to be reconciled and then forget about the problem—they were going to expend the effort to make it happen.

---

19   Ibid., p. 86.

With this very admirable goal, they organized a reconciliation conference in the central location of Ohnenheim, a village in
the Alsace just a few miles from where Jakob Ammann probably
lived.[20] Here, the Anabaptists had been tolerated for decades. The
town's mill was owned by an Anabaptist who had been legally
holding church meetings there for many years. In fact, 34 years
earlier, this was the very mill where thirteen Swiss Brethren ministers had signed the Dortrecht Confession of Faith! The date for
the conference was set for March 12, 1694. Ten delegates, nine
of them ministers, came from Switzerland. Among them were
Hans Reist and Peter Giger. Seven Palatine ministers came. An
unknown number of Amish ministers came.[21]

At the meeting, the Palatines listened carefully to both the
Reistians and the Amish, as they later came to be called.[22] After
carefully investigating the situation, the Palatines begged the
Amish to not act too rashly.[23]

Despite the sincere effort, peace could not be made. The Amish
brought up the three main issues that concerned them—shunning,
the Truehearted, and the excommunication of liars. The Reistians
refused to agree with the Amish on any of these points.

The Palatines, however, expressed agreement with Ammann on
the excommunication of liars and not consoling the Truehearted as

---

20   He probably was living somewhere in southern Alsace, although exactly where is unknown.

21   Ulli Ammann, "Summary and Defense," in Roth, p. 88; Christian Blank, "Summary and
Defense," in Roth, p. 117; Hans Reist et al., "Statement from Ohnenheim," in Roth, p. 48.

22   At this point in the story, we will switch to using these two names for the two parties of
the division. Maybe it is not fair to characterize the division after the two leading personalities
when in fact many men were involved, but history has definitely denominated the one side as
"Amish." To make it fair, we will now call the other side the "Reistians." However, we need
to keep in mind that many other people played important roles, some of them probably even
unnamed and unknown.

23   Christian Blank, "Summary and Defense," in Roth, p. 117.

saved. However, they could not agree with Ammann on making every congregation and individual take on the Amish view of shunning. One of the Palatines, Jakob Gut, asked Ammann to observe shunning according to his own understanding and not impose it on others.[24] Some other minor points of disagreement with the Amish seem to have come up, but what they were has not been discovered. Having failed to reach any agreement, the meeting ended for the night, and the Amish ministers went home.

The next day, the Reistians met with the Palatine ministers in the mill once again. None of the Amish were present. At this second meeting, the Palatines told the Reistians that if they "did not want to confess the two articles regarding the Truehearted and those who tell lies," the Palatines "could be just as little satisfied with them as Jakob Ammann was satisfied with them."[25]

On hearing this, all nine of the Reistian ministers suddenly decided to agree with the Palatines on the issues of the excommunication of liars and the Truehearted!

Imagine! One day they say that they do not agree with two issues, then the next day they do a total 180° turn and say they do!

Now that the Reistians had suddenly decided to agree with the Palatines, they proceeded to draw up a written statement together:

A statement from us, the ministers and elders from the Palatinate and Switzerland regarding the articles about which we cannot agree with Jakob Ammann. This is the reason: he introduced shunning in daily eating and drinking on the basis of 1 Corinthians, Chapter 5, and not content with this alone, he also excommunicates from the fellowship all those who do not confess this with him and portrays them as deceitful, apostate, heretical, and rabble-rousers. Therefore

24   Jakob Gut, "Jakob Gut to the Congregation at Baldenheim," in Roth, p. 52.

25   Ulli Ammann, "Summary and Defense," in Roth, p. 88.

we cannot and do not desire to consider him and all those who stand with him as brothers and sisters, for in our understanding of shunning we do not acknowledge that the apostle in I Corinthians 5 wrote about daily eating but rather of the Passover lamb which is Christ crucified for us. . . . To strengthen this affirmation, we give you the assurance of those of us, the undersigned ministers and elders from the Palatinate and Switzerland. Signed on March 13, 1694 at Ohnen in the mill.[26]

With this document, they excommunicated *en masse* all the Amish side—not only the ministers who had been involved in the trouble, but all of them—men, women, and youth alike, with no apparent attempt at admonishing them individually for their supposed errors, as the Amish had done with them. Furthermore, unlike Ammann's "Warning Letter," there is no request directed to the other side to show the document's signers a better way from God's Word, if possible.

These actions had a further effect. By placing the blame for the disturbance on the sole issue of shunning, the Reistians were able to perform a cunning sleight-of-hand, making it appear that the entire trouble was about a single doctrinal issue about which there was a difference of opinion. They made it appear that the whole fuss happened because Ammann "introduced" the practice and excommunicated all those who disagreed. There is no mention of the other two points (about which the Palatines also rebuked the Reistians), about the Truehearted and liars, which would have shown that at least some Reistians had compromised the clear line between the church and the world (by comforting the Truehearted) and had compromised church purity (by refusing to

---

26   Hans Reist et al., "Statement from Ohnenheim," in Roth, pp. 47-48.

discipline liars). This had the effect of making Ammann and his group look like simple troublemakers, rather than people concerned about the purity of the church.[27]

In response to this, Jakob Ammann and those who supported him excommunicated the Palatine ministers.[28]

Summary

By this point, the Reistians were showing attitudes and actions that went beyond the poor attitudes that the Amish had shown. Yes, the Amish had excommunicated several ministers without the counsel of the whole congregation. Guess what the Reistians and Palatines just did? Exactly the same!

Yes, the Amish had acted rashly in trying to get everyone across the brotherhood to practice social shunning just like they did, and when someone disagreed, they were excommunicated after at least two personal warnings. Guess what? Now the Reistians and Palatines were excommunicating people who happened to disagree with *their* view of shunning—not only individuals, but whole congregations, very few of which they had personally admonished before!

So it is that the Reistians (and the Palatines) showed their true colors. There were hints of this before, with the Emmentaler ministers who changed opinions over the course of a few days, but now it was plainer yet. Something was at work in their midst—something besides the work of the Holy Ghost.

---

27   While there is no way to say which of the issues was the most important to Ammann himself, it is noteworthy that he devoted much more space to the issue of the Truehearted in his "Long Letter" than he gave to the issue of shunning.

28   Christian Blank, "Summary and Defense," in Roth, p. 117. Some of the Palatine ministers mentioned having been excommunicated by Ammann, including Jakob Gut (Roth, p. 53), and Hans-Rudolf Nägeli (Roth, p. 57).

In 1694-5, many Anabaptists left Steffisburg (pictured here) and moved to Ste. Marie-aux-Mines in northern Alsace.

CHAPTER 8

Captured!

n the year 1694, the Anabaptist communities in the Oberland—and Jakob Ammann as one of their leaders—faced a dilemma. The tolerant *Landvogt* (governor), Karl Manuel, had died in 1692. With their protector gone, the Anabaptists faced the possibility of newly increased persecution. A wave of new anti-Anabaptist decrees was passed by the Bern Council in 1693-1694. Could they flee to Alsace, where some of their brethren had already gone?

They could not move to the Rhine Valley in southern Alsace. There, local authorities had set limits for the number of Anabaptists allowed to settle in their territories, and those limits were being met and exceeded. A different solution had to be found.

In the spring/summer of 1694, Jakob traveled down to the Oberland area with the apparent goal of finding a way to help his people out of Switzerland. (Alternately, he may have stayed in Switzerland over the winter, managing to avoid capture.)

The Bern government had not given up watching for Jakob—it still considered him a highly wanted "arch-Anabaptist." In July, they caught him! Not only that, they also caught his co-minister,

Peter Zimmerman.

Ammann was captured by the *Landvogt* of Trachselwald in the village of Walkringen, which was about six miles east of Bern on the road between Thun and Burgdorf (avoiding the capital city). When arrested, he was carrying at least one letter, intended for the Dutch Anabaptists. Who wrote the letter and what it said remain a mystery, as no copy of the letter has been discovered. The official turned Jakob over to three local men for safekeeping. These three—possibly "Truehearted"—promptly allowed Jakob to escape.

Needless to say, the release of this highly-wanted individual was not pleasing to the lords of Bern. The provincial governor of Thorberg promptly gave an order for the three who released Ammann to be arrested.

Ammann's escape was fortunate. If he had been successfully detained and imprisoned, he faced the possibility of a long prison stay and potentially even a galley sentence. Peter Zimmerman was taken to Bern and imprisoned there. In October, he escaped.

Despite the arrests, the Anabaptists of Steffisburg found the solution they were looking for. The state church pastor at Steffisburg, Hans Jacob Freudenreich (1639-1710), was a congenial man who knew the Anabaptists well. Over the span of a few short years, the Anabaptists of Steffisburg streamed out of Switzerland. Not only were they allowed to leave, they were allowed to leave with their children and possessions. As icing on the cake, the customary 10% Abzuggelt (export tax) was, at least for some, reduced to 5%. How did they get such privileges?

Some historians have speculated that Jakob, while in Switzerland, negotiated with the authorities, using Pastor Freudenreich as an intermediary. With such favorable terms, the Anabaptists could leave intolerant Bern and the Bernese authorities would be permanently

The galleys

A 16th-century galley ship.

Had Jakob Ammann remained in custody and been brought to prison in Bern, there is a very real possibility he would have been sentenced to galley slavery.

Considered one of the most terrible sentences possible, galley slaves were chained to a bench in the hold of a galley ship, forced to row hour after hour. They were horribly maltreated, often being whipped or beaten for little or no reason, rowing, rowing, rowing, all day, every day—until they died.

For Anabaptist prisoners, the challenge was greater. Not only were the companions ungodly, the work grueling, and the maltreatment extreme, but the galley ships were often warships, which the nonresistant could not help to row.

The history of galleys goes all the way back to ancient Egypt, but by the 1600s, they were nearly outdated. They were not very seaworthy in storms, and with the advent of cannons, the galley's combat usefulness became limited. The French still used them, and they were rowed by criminals, Muslims, and Huguenots (French

Protestants). Following Louis XIV's revocation of the Edict of Nantes (which guaranteed religious liberty to Protestants in France), many Huguenots were forced into galley slavery.

Protestant Zürich sent Anabaptist prisoners to the Catholic French and Italians to serve as galley slaves. In 1659, Bern's Täuferkammer (Anabaptist Chamber) ruled that Anabaptist prisoners should not be sent to the French as galley slaves, but it still happened occasionally—in 1671, six were sent to the galleys, and more in 1714 and 1717. Due to intercession from other Swiss and the Dutch, the groups sentenced in 1714 and 1717 were recalled.

While the Bernese government was incensed over the French Catholics' persecution of Huguenots, they did not see such righteous indignation as being inconsistent with their own persecution of Anabaptists, or even (occasionally) with sending those Anabaptists to the French for punishment in the galleys!

rid of a large group of annoying Anabaptists.[1]

The result was that an influx of Anabaptists came to the Alsatian mining town of Ste. Marie-aux-Mines (pronounced Sont-maree-oh-meen, meaning "St. Mary of the Mines"), also known by the German name of Markirch.

Ste. Marie was a mining town with a long history. Silver was discovered there in the tenth century, over 600 years before Jakob Ammann arrived there. In the 1500s, 3,000 miners arrived in the area in only a few decades; mining at Markirch was at its peak. Under the rule of the lords of Ribeaupierre from the Palatinate, the area had embraced the Reformation in the sixteenth century.

---

1   Robert Baecher, "From Steffisburg to Ste. Marie-aux-Mines: The Exodus of Those Who Would Become Amish, Part II," *Mennonite Family History* 23(2) (April 2004):69-81, pp. 77-81.

Ste. Marie-aux-Mines, new home for Oberlander Anabaptists.

During the Thirty Years' War, France took control of Alsace, but the Treaty of Münster prevented the fanatically Catholic French King Louis XIV from banishing Protestantism from Alsace. To the contrary, the Anabaptists continued to find toleration in Alsace.

In 1673, Alsace passed under the rule of the Birkenfeld family. Christian II, Palatine Count of Birkenfeld, was a Protestant and had Pietist tendencies (he had been a student of the famous Pietist leader, Philip Jakob Spener). He continued to favor the Anabaptists in Alsace.

While the Thirty Years' War did not destroy Protestantism in the region, it did severely disrupt the area. The mines fell into disuse since so many miners had died. At war's end, the lords wanted farmers to restore the region to productivity once again, and Bernese Anabaptists began to migrate to Alsace.

Anabaptists had lived in Ste. Marie since the 1500s, but more came in the aftermath of the Thirty Years' War. The Amish migration in 1694 was another wave, which helped to bring farms into bountiful production.

Jakob Ammann's house in the Ste. Marie-aux-Mines valley.

CHAPTER 9

Home in the Valley

ometime around 1694 or 1695, Jakob Ammann himself moved to Ste. Marie-aux-Mines, where a number of members of the Anabaptist congregation from Steffisburg had settled. Jakob ended up living in a remote place near the end of the valley called Petite Lièpvre, near Echery. Here he spent many long years in fruitful service to his people. He came to be called—by the government officials at least—the "Patriarche" of the Anabaptists.[1]

To the Alsace!

As described in the last chapter, many Anabaptists left Steffisburg in the early 1690s for the Ste. Marie-aux-Mines valley. Christian III, Palatine Count and ruler of Alsace, was a Protestant with Pietist sympathies and was tolerant of the Anabaptists. Upon the arrival of the refugees, the local Reformed pastor led an effort by his Huguenot (French Reformed) congregation to provide

---

1   The exact reason they used this term is not known. Ammann was probably the most prominent leader in the area, and was often a spokesman for the Anabaptists in their interactions with the local government. The term seems to acknowledge his status as an important leader.

The Ste. Marie valley.

temporary lodging for the newcomers. They stayed in the school, in the houses of local residents, at least one stayed in a barn, and one stayed in the home of Chancellor Fattet, a high-ranking local government official.

Many of the Anabaptists—immigrants though they were—had sufficient sums of money to be able to buy large farms in the region. They began to make the valley productive again.

Michel Passes On

Meanwhile, back in Heidolsheim, death struck. In the midst of all the responsibilities of moving an entire congregation across international borders and the ongoing controversy with the Reistians, Jakob's own father Michel—who had embraced the faith which his sons were so zealously defending—died in Heidolsheim in April 1695 at the age of 79.

Now there was a problem. The local Catholic church would not allow Michel to be buried in the town. He was finally buried in Baldenheim at the Reformed Church, where a tolerant pastor permitted it. Michel's death record reads as follows:

> On Saturday, the 23rd of April [1695] a non-resident Anabaptist of the name of Michl Amme—a tailor by trade from Steffisburg—was buried here since this was refused him at Heidolsheim where he died.[2]

Shepherd in the Valley

It did not take long for the Anabaptists and their leader to attract some attention. In 1696, the *Landrichter* (provincial judge) investigated Jakob and wrote a report:

> The one named Jacob Ammann, leader of the new Anabaptist sect, commonly called 'the Patriarch,' is a man against whom we have no complaints. Since he is in this jurisdiction, he has conducted himself in a most obedient and respectful way to the orders of the king and officers of the town. . . . This [behavior] he also has inspired in all those of his sect who have conducted themselves in the same manner. This man does not own anything, no farm, and we cannot tell by what means he exists—if it is by means of a pension that those from the sect or any other give to him.[3]

Of course, Jakob earned his income by tailoring, which did not require any land, but the *Landrichter* had no way of telling how Jakob earned his bread.

Not everyone in the valley who dealt with Jakob was so positive about him. The local Catholic priest, a man named Laforest, was

---

2   Robert Baecher, "The 'Patriarche' of Sainte-Marie-aux-Mines," *Mennonite Quarterly Review* 74(1) (January 2000):145-158, pp. 146-147.

3   Ibid., pp. 155-156.

as passionately Catholic as Ammann was passionately Anabaptist. The combination of the two strong characters in one valley was bound to create friction if they clashed.

Laforest was the priest of the St. Louis Catholic Church in Ste. Marie. After the Thirty Years' War, there were few Catholics in the valley and the mass was not being held in the area. In 1673, the King of France, Louis XIV, promised to give government money to establish a parish there. Laforest became the first priest of the new church.

With the flood of Anabaptist refugees, Laforest determined that he was losing income. After all, each Anabaptist in the area meant one less dwelling place available for a Catholic who would pay for the priest's religious services of baptism, marriage, etc. Laforest wrote to the priests of Ohnenheim and Ste. Croix, inquiring about the amounts that they received from Anabaptists in their areas as a sort of "tax" to replace lost income. He adopted their prices as his own, and declared that the Anabaptists living in his parish "are to begin paying their dues beginning January 1, 1696." He wanted to charge a flat rate of 30 sols per household per year, plus fees for deaths, marriages, births, and to supply communion bread for the parish—this in spite of the fact that, of course, the Anabaptists would not require or even want the priest's services on these occasions. Nevertheless, the priests at Ohnenheim and Ste. Croix received their money from the Anabaptists and so did Laforest—for a brief while.

Before long, the Prince learned of Laforest's actions, and he was not happy about the matter. Laforest wrote a letter to the Prince on March 9, 1696, saying:

> I confess and repent of committing a grave mistake which, contrary to my wishes, may have angered Your Most Serene Highness. But

Jakob Ammann's house in Alsace. The lighter-colored part to the left is a later addition.

I promise I would be committing an even greater sin if I despaired of receiving a pardon from my Prince, pardon which God Himself refuses to no one and which no man could refuse in good conscience, especially in promising as I promise to henceforth be more circumspect in all that regards to the Interdicts[4] of His Highness.[5]

Nevertheless, just a few months later, Laforest again attempted to have the Anabaptists forced to pay him the fees he wanted. On October 7, 1696, he wrote the following letter to the Prince's Councilor, Fattet:

Sir, as I am honored to be a servant to all, I am eager to give you this word of notice in writing rather than orally so that it will not

---

4   Prohibitions.

5   Jean Séguy, "The Bernese Anabaptists in Sainte-Marie-aux-Mines," *Pennsylvania Mennonite Heritage* 3(3) (July 1980):2-9, pp. 8-9.

escape your memory and so you can faithfully communicate it to whomever you please.

Notice is hereby given that I have received numerous complaints which have some semblance of truth. The first involves defiance of the King's edict which explicitly states that no one from any religion other than Roman Catholic should be received into my parish; nevertheless, there is a daily influx of Anabaptists who number nearly sixty families and who occupy land that could be used by Catholics. I thus request the right to charge the Anabaptists the same fees, as much for deaths as for marriages, just as though they were my Catholic parishioners. These fees are the same as those that they pay at Onesme [Ohnenheim] and at Ste. Croix. If not, I will have them expelled. Secondly, the people of your religion are giving all the work [i.e., leasing] to Anabaptists so that the Catholics, having no means of subsistence, will be obliged to leave. Thus I am obliged to warn against your measures, since the intention of His Majesty was not to build the Church of St. Louis in order to banish the Catholics while tolerating the Anabaptists, and I will not suffer them. . . .

You are aware of the duties and obligations of a true Roman Catholic priest like myself. In a word, I will not suffer anything that could be contrary to my religion. Your affectionate: The Priest of St. Louis.[6]

Councillor Fattet refused to grant Laforest his request. At this, Laforest brought his complaints before the Sovereign Council of Alsace, apparently with no better result. He had no choice but to give up on receiving the money—although he did not give up his opposition to the Anabaptists in general and Jakob Ammann in

---

6   Ibid., p. 9.

particular. He wrote, "As for me, I cannot bear them!"[7]

Although his attempts to get the Anabaptists to pay him had been thwarted, Laforest continued to oppose the Anabaptists. Late in 1696, he attempted to convert at least one Amish woman to Catholicism. He had visited Christian Kropf's wife and used intimidation and threats to try to force her to convert. She was apparently so frightened by the event that she was ill in bed after the priest's visit. Jakob Ammann seems to have thought such conduct was unbecoming of a minister and confronted Laforest in the village street. He told the priest that he would let the authorities know of the incident. Evidently Laforest had threatened to "take care of the so-called Jacquy Aman." Jakob ended up making a complaint to the authorities about the over-zealous methods of the priest, and they apparently ruled in favor of the Anabaptists.[8]

Reclaiming Nonresistance

Early in 1696, Jakob Ammann worked out an agreement for militia exemption between the Anabaptists and the government. It appears that the former Anabaptist inhabitants (and perhaps even some of the members of Ammann's congregation) had compromised by serving in the militia or in the *Heimburg*, a local elected political office mostly responsible for collecting taxes. On February 27, 1696, Jakob Ammann "of the Anabaptist religion" appeared before the Provost of Ste. Marie. He came "in the name of all those of his religion living in the entire Valley, whither they had come about two years ago" and informed the provost that the Amish "were not in a position to have one single member serve as Heimburg in any

---

7 Robert Baecher, "The 'Patriarche' of Sainte-Marie-aux-Mines," *Mennonite Quarterly Review* 74(1) (January 2000)74(1) (January 2000):145-158, p. 149.

8 Robert Baecher, "The 'Patriarche' of Sainte-Marie-aux-Mines," *Mennonite Quarterly Review* 74(1) (January 2000):145-158, p. 152.

area of this Valley, or for their young men to serve in the militia, as they previously had done."

Jakob was firm and uncompromising, but he was also reasonable. In exchange for the privilege of exemption, he offered "to pay a few signs of good will each year for being relieved of duties as Heimburg and in the militia." The provost granted their request, exempting the Anabaptists on condition that they pay a fee of 55 tournois per year. Jakob agreed to the conditions and paid the fine.[9]

Heartbreak in the Valley

In October 1697, tragedy struck the Amish community of Ste. Marie. Peter Zimmerman, one of their elders and owner of a sawmill, was doing fall cleanup in the fields when his deafness kept him from hearing a large log rolling down a hill toward him. Hans Weiss, a fellow Amishman, had cut down the tree—obviously without intending to hit Peter. The log hit Peter on the side, severely injuring him, and not too long after, he passed away.

A few members of the Amish community were present at the hastily-arranged funeral. They buried Peter at the edge of a row of trees at La Petite Lièpvre, wrapped in a burial cloth. When the local police heard of the event, they began an investigation and exhumed Zimmerman, then performed an autopsy. The investigation ended with Jakob Ammann and several of Peter's relatives rehearsing the story to the authorities and assuring them that the death was purely accidental. All concerned had forgiven poor Hans Weiss.[10]

9   Jean Séguy, "The Bernese Anabaptists in Sainte-Marie-aux-Mines," *Pennsylvania Mennonite Heritage* 3(3) (July 1980):2-9, pp. 5-6.

10   Robert Baecher, "The 'Patriarche' of Sainte-Marie-aux-Mines," *Mennonite Quarterly Review* 74(1) (January 2000):145-158, p. 153; Robert Baecher, "From Steffisburg to Ste. Marie-aux-Mines: The Exodus of Those Who Would Become Amish, Part I," *Mennonite Family History* 23(1) (January 2004):4-16, p. 15.

You Cannot Have Our Children!

Jakob cared for those of his congregation and was not at all hesitant to petition the government when his people's welfare was at stake. This was not a protest against the government, but a request for his people to be protected from those who would take advantage of them. In 1701, the Amish congregation faced just such a situation.

An Amish brother whose wife was a member of the state church died.[11] After his death, the clerk of Ste. Marie immediately claimed the right to "take inventory of their [the deceased's] possessions, liquidate their estates, and appoint guardians for those of the children whose parents were deceased." Accordingly, the clerk ordered an inventory and tried to put the orphan children under the guardianship of their home town in Switzerland. Jakob, on the other hand, wanted the children to have Amish guardians. He, along with "Preacher" Jacob Hochstetler and Hans Zimmerman, wrote a petition to the Prince. Jakob pointed out that such actions as the clerk had undertaken were in opposition "to their [the Anabaptists'] privileges which the Lord [Prince] had granted them and for which they had paid a protection right."[12] Jakob threatened that if the case was not decided in favor of the Anabaptists, he would "move his stake somewhere else."

The case was assigned to Grand Bailiff Bartemann, who rebuked the village clerk and ordered him to stop his investigations. He also ordered that the children should be provided with tutors and that the Amish congregation would be allowed to continue "according to their customary procedures."[13]

---

11   This does not mean that he had married outside the Amish church, but likely that he had married and then converted. Remember, these are mostly first-generation Anabaptists. Such situations were fairly common among the Swiss Brethren.

12   Jean Séguy, "The Bernese Anabaptists in Sainte-Marie-aux-Mines," *Pennsylvania Mennonite Heritage* 3(3) (July 1980):2-9, p. 6.

13   Robert Baecher, "The 'Patriarche' of Sainte-Marie-aux-Mines," *Mennonite Quarterly*

How did the early Amish dress?

Unfortunately, we have very little information about Swiss Anabaptist clothing from the late 17th and early 18th centuries, when Jakob Ammann was active as an Anabaptist leader. From Ammann's own pen, we have only this statement about clothing and grooming:

> If there would be someone who wants to be conformed to the world with shaved beard, with long hair, and haughty clothing and does not acknowledge that it is wrong, he should in all fairness be punished. For God has no pleasure in the proud.[1]

This shows that Ammann considered a shaved beard, long hair, and "haughty" clothing to be evidences of pride. We can conclude that he dressed in a plain way compared to contemporary cultural norms, grew a beard, and had short hair (although how short is impossible to say). He probably did not shave his mustache, however, as that tradition seems to have begun in the early 1800s.

We do have artistic portrayals of Anabaptists from the early 1800s. They show fairly consistent forms of clothing for Swiss/French Anabaptists of this time period, and may represent forms of dress similar to what would have been worn earlier.

In 1702, a Catholic priest described the Amish of Ste. Marie-aux-Mines as having long beards and both men and women wearing linen. We do know

---

1   Jakob Ammann, "Summary and Defense," in Roth, p. 40.

that Swiss Anabaptists of Ammann's day wore some kind of distinctive dress. Hans Hornley, an Amish shoemaker in Ste. Marie, made shoes "only for those of like faith whose shoes had to be made over a special pattern."[2] What that pattern was, we do not know.

Georg Thormann, a Reformed pastor writing in 1693 (the year in which the Amish dispute began), said that the Swiss Anabaptists "wear no collars around the neck, no fur trim or lace, or what is commonly regarded as fancy clothing worn pridefully."[3] He indicated they were distinctive in their attire, but besides these three things they did not wear, he did not explain what about their attire made them distinctive.

In 1568, the Swiss Brethren elders gathered in Strasbourg wrote:

Tailors and seamstresses shall hold to the plain and simple style and shall make nothing at all for pride's sake. The brethren and sisters shall remain steadfastly by the present standard of our regulations concerning apparel, and shall make nothing for pride's sake. Furthermore, shaving off the beard or trimming the hair of the head in stylish ways shall not be permitted.[4]

Sadly, the text of the "present standard of our regulations" to which the elders refer has not survived.

---

2   Robert Baecher, "The 'Patriarche' of Sainte-Marie-aux-Mines," *Mennonite Quarterly Review* 74(1) (January 2000):145-158, p. 156.

3   George Thormann, *Probier-Stein*, translated by Katharina Epp, 2005, p. 475.

4   Strasbourg Discipline, Article 20; translation from William R. McGrath, editor, *Christlicher Ordnung or Christian Discipline*, 1966, Pathway Publishing, p. 15.

Tax Troubles

Soon after arriving in the Markirch Valley, Jakob Ammann had worked out the terms of the Anabaptists' military/*Heimburg* exemption with the government officials. The agreed-upon fee was reassessed every three years. In 1696, it was 45 pounds, and in 1699 it went down to 39, but in 1702 it rose sharply to 90 pounds. The government authorities apparently tried to make some more money on their conscientious subjects; in addition, they proposed that the Anabaptists "[take] care of the past" by paying an additional 210 pounds.

Representing his community, Jakob Ammann met with the local fiscal officer on February 28, 1701. He complained about the idea of "taking care of the past" with a large sum of money, pointed out the instructions of a higher government official, and threatened to leave the area. In response, the fiscal officer wrote to Counselor Scheid, a counselor to the Prince of Birkenfeld. He pointed out that the Anabaptists had "restored many farms and much of the land of the valley" and that they "do not quibble or cause the slightest chicanery[14] and they pay well." The Anabaptists seem to have received their request, but it was not to be the end of their tax troubles.

In late 1701 or early 1702, the inhabitants of Ste. Marie-aux-Mines complained to the higher officials about the Anabaptists' exemption from the *Heimburg*. The government used the opportunity to raise the Anabaptists' exemption fee by making them pay separately for exemption from military service and from the Heimburg. Although the Anabaptists tried to get this dropped, they ended up paying 45 pounds more for exemption. This did not

---

Review 74(1) (January 2000):145-158, p. 153.

14   Subtlety or trickery.

settle the issue for the non-Anabaptist inhabitants of Markirch, and they would eventually protest again.[15]

Standing Against Deception

In 1707, a Lutheran girl by the name of Elizabeth seriously considered converting to Roman Catholicism. A man named Claude Didier gave Elizabeth a ride in his carriage from La Petite Lièpvre to priest Laforest's house in Ste. Marie-aux-Mines. However, Elizabeth's Anabaptist uncle, Maurice Luthi, soon heard of what was happening and came running as fast as he could to catch up with her. When he did, he caught her by the arm and said: "You have no business going to Monsieur le cure [the Priest]. He is not the one who is your master. I am the one who is!" Maurice then took his niece to the Anabaptist sawmill owner, Christian Kropf, and then to Jakob Ammann—who was later described in the court record as *"Aman Jacky*, the patriarch of the so-called Anabaptists." Kropf and Ammann allegedly convinced Elizabeth that "if she becomes a Catholic she would be lost."

Laforest apparently complained to the government about the incident, and the Alsatian officials investigated. Maurice Luthi denied the accusations. The investigation was ended when the vicar-general acknowledged that Luthi had not merited any punishment even if the story was true.[16]

The Locals Complain Again

In early 1708, the Anabaptists requested—probably in a routine manner—that their exemption rights be renewed. The local

15   Jean Séguy, "The Bernese Anabaptists in Sainte-Marie-aux-Mines," *Pennsylvania Mennonite Heritage* 3(3) (July 1980):2-9, pp. 6-7.

16   Robert Baecher, "The 'Patriarche' of Sainte-Marie-aux-Mines," *Mennonite Quarterly Review* 74(1) (January 2000):145-158, pp. 152-153.

non-Anabaptist population complained and wrote a petition to the Prince dated January 31, 1708. They asserted that the Anabaptists' exemption was an "unjust right" which obligated the rest of the Valley's inhabitants to do guard duty more often than it was their turn.[17] They claimed that "this cannot continue without totally ruining the poor suppliants." They also claimed that a number of the local Anabaptists "have not raised any objection to serving or to having someone serve in their place, even the most recently arrived [the Amish] who are the most obstinate." They asked that the Prince give an order "that the Anabaptists be subject to the same and similar duties as your own natural subjects."[18]

It appears that the Prince never responded to the petition, and the locals tried again in August 1708. This time they addressed their petition to Monsieur Bartemann, the Grand Bailiff of Ribeaupierre. They said:

> It is entirely impossible for them to continue to march or to be ready at any moment to take arms if the Anabaptists, who are settled in large numbers in these areas, are not likewise obliged to march with them, which would be even more just and reasonable since it is for their protection just as much as for the suppliants. This considered, Sir, may it please you to order these Anabaptists to march and to be prepared at all times to bear arms just like the suppliants, or if they prefer, find other men to replace them.[19]

Bartemann ordered that the Anabaptists give a reply to the

---

17   This, of course, was true. Since everyone was supposed to take his turn at guard duty, if 25% (the estimated population of Anabaptists in the valley) did not take a turn, then the rest would have to do 25% more duty than normal.

18   Jean Séguy, "The Bernese Anabaptists in Sainte-Marie-aux-Mines," *Pennsylvania Mennonite Heritage* 3(3) (July 1980):2-9, p. 7.

19   Ibid.

Jakob Ammann's memory lives on in Ste. Marie, with a road named after him.

petition within two weeks. A copy was given to them, but any reply they gave has now been lost. Nothing was ever done about the complaints.[20]

Summary

Jakob Ammann had an active, but little-known, ministry in the region of Ste. Marie-aux-Mines. The Anabaptists there enjoyed a very unique political situation. Their skills and contributions to the royal treasury through tax revenue and exemption fees made them important inhabitants whom the government was eager to please. Therefore, Jakob could ask for nearly anything and get what he wanted!

Jakob is still remembered in the area. The main road leading into Ste. Marie-aux-Mines, formerly called Petite Lièpvre, has recently been renamed "Rue Jacob Amann"—"Jakob Ammann Road."

While Jakob was caring for his flock in the Markirch area, important attempts were being made to bring about a reconciliation between the Amish and Reistian factions of the Swiss Brethren.

---

20   Ibid.

CHAPTER 10

Peace at Last?

lthough the Amish ministers were zealous to see the church cleansed of error and sin, they—particularly Ulli Ammann—were also zealous to see the broken peace restored. They initiated several attempts to bring about a reconciliation between the two groups. Some of these attempts we have no details about, but we do have records of others.

The Controversy Continues

The Ohnenheim Reconciliation Conference did not end the controversy between the two sides. Obviously, playing church politics does not heal church divisions; it makes them worse.

Several letters were exchanged between the various parties, particularly from the Palatines, defending the divergent points of view. In particular, the Reistians defended their views regarding shunning and attacked Jakob Ammann personally. The Amish had used words like "liar, apostate, heretic, and trouble-maker," and now it was their turn to get some of the same back—with compound interest. Jakob was a liar, gossiper, ranter, Diotrephes (whom John warned about in his Third Epistle), and even the horseman who robs the earth of peace described in the Revelation of John! He was a fallen star and demon-possessed.[1] Jakob just wanted a big following, one Reistian claimed, while another said he promised salvation to anyone who would agree with him.

Not only was Jakob an evil character, he was accused of making social shunning to be the source of salvation, rather than salvation by "the merit of Christ." Social shunning was becoming a "source of serious idolatry," since supposedly Jakob said one could not be saved without it; he was making it to be "the abomination in the holy place."[2]

On the Reistian side, accusations went from bad to worse. Since the church politics game had started back at Ohnenheim, it seems that attitudes were growing nastier with each move.

On the other hand—once the name-calling is overlooked—the Palatine ministers made more cogent arguments against social shunning than the Emmentaler Reistians gave at the beginning of the quarrel. Instead of quoting verses about not being defiled with food going in the mouth, they began giving reasons why Paul meant communion when he said "with such an one no not to eat." While that position is debatable, it was at least a better starting point, but the hard words drowned out the rational arguments.

An Encounter with Jakob

Letters containing the accusations and arguments appear to have been copied, recopied, and distributed for the "edification" of all who wished to read them. Jakob Ammann heard that Peter Lehman and Rudolf Hauser, the ministers of a Züricher Anabaptist group in Alsace, had carried such letters to Switzerland. Jakob apparently

---

1   Ulli Ammann, "Summary and Defense," in Roth, pp. 90-91. Ulli was not exaggerating— several of these expressions can be found in the Reistians' letters.

2   Hans-Rudolf Nägeli, "Hans-Rudolf Nägeli, et al. to Hans Reist," in Roth, pp. 72, 74.

asked them to meet him at a certain meetinghouse. The meeting was a failure, to say the least.

Hauser and Lehman arrived at the meetinghouse and Jakob asked Peter to read the letters aloud. Peter began with Jakob Gut's letter. When he finished, a heated argument erupted, which went something like this:

Jakob: "You have carried deceitful letters into Switzerland, have gone to those congregations, read them aloud, and made the churches I am responsible for turn away from me."

Another Amish man: "You should quit, or Jakob will have to do what is necessary in the matter. He wants to have you warned another time. If you will not quit, Jakob will have to take other means to resolve the matter."

Hauser and Lehman: "You are not going to intimidate us; we will not relinquish our offices."

Jakob: "You are false teachers, banned, deceitful men, and the Devil's servants."

Peter Lehman: "I don't know which false doctrine I have taught."

Jakob: "You renounced shunning."

Peter Lehman: "We want to shun you, because you are worth shunning."

Jakob: "I have no desire to have anything to do with you. If I had one hair on my head that would desire it, I would rip it out."

Jakob then asked Peter to read another letter. He began to read Jonas Lohr's letter, but when he reached the part where Lohr challenged Ammann to prove shunning, the quarreling began again —"just as if fire had gotten into straw, with scoldings and insults like I have hardly ever heard," Peter Lehman later wrote. Jakob scolded, "Be ashamed of yourselves, you old gray heads, you liars and reprobates."[3] The argument began again with fresh vigor when the two sides disagreed about the ownership of a certain meetinghouse.

Unfortunately, we have no record of Ammann's side of the story, and we do not know if Lehman's account is accurate.

Nevertheless, it seems clear that both sides engaged in heated argumentation and name-calling that was totally out of place. We are left to wonder: If the meeting had been spent seeking peace and reconciliation with humility and prayer, what progress may have been made?

Concern for Peace

Despite continued controversy, some on both sides—including Jakob Ammann—were eager to work towards a reconciliation. They did not want to think that the division would be permanent. This in itself seems to indicate that perhaps the Reistian version of the story above is not a fair presentation of how things went.

In the meantime, two of the Palatine ministers who had signed the Ohnenheim agreement—Hans Gut and Christian Holly—examined the controversy more closely and realized with remorse what they had helped to do at Ohnenheim. In acknowledgment of their fault, they excommunicated themselves from the church and later began to support the Amish.

The importance of this move by these two humble men can hardly be understated. The importance is *not* which side they left or joined, but that they simply had the humility to say something no one in the division had said until now: We were wrong, and we are sorry. Please forgive us!

Hallelujah! How the angels must have rejoiced to see men willing to admit mistakes! Maybe peace was possible after all!

---

3   Peter Lehman and Rudolf Hauser, in Roth, p. 79.

Meetings for Peace

Many meetings were called in an attempt to make peace. Ulli Ammann wrote later:

> There were, however, on both sides calls to restore the peace which has been broken. We also hoped to be reunited in faith. I can say with a clear conscience that all this has caused me great pain and has been heavy on my heart. This is why people went around in the Palatinate, in Alsace and in Switzerland and met many times. But it happened every time that when we thought the conference was going to be well-attended, and the brothers and sisters on their side who were most desirous of peace would also be there, then they were kept back every time. They were allowed to come to us only rarely, and then those ministers came who cared little about peace. It was the intention on our side to see first if we could unite again in faith, which was the reason the quarrel had begun. But if we spoke about matters of faith, then they began to speak of our mistakes and even if they confessed the faith with us, we had supposedly still treated them badly in this and they took action against us because of those words and hasty judgments. . . .[4]

More Humility!

Incredibly, the story of humility and repentance did not end with the two Palatine ministers; it spread. Against the backdrop of heated emotions and escalating rhetoric, something incredible happened: The Amish side became convinced that they, in spite of their good intentions, had failed to manifest a Christian attitude in the matter. Maybe the names that they were being called helped them to realize the carnality of the name-calling that they had been

---

4   Ulli Ammann, "Summary and Defense," in Roth, p. 91.

involved in. They agreed on the following points:

1. They should have asked brotherhood approval before excommunicating the Emmental ministers.
2. They had acted too rashly and should have had more patience.
3. They still believed that their doctrinal points were true and that the Emmental ministers had merited discipline, but they acknowledged that they did not carry out the excommunication procedure as blamelessly as they should have.
4. Even though the others had given cause for it, they should not have called the Emmental ministers "liars, quarrelers, apostates, and rabble-rousers" since these terms served more to offend than enlighten.

Ulli wrote, "Even if we were given cause, however, and since many people cannot understand these names well, finding them to be more repulsive and to serve as a hindrance rather than a way of correcting others, we have now recognized and believe that it would have been better to avoid these and to use other, more moderate words."[5]

Oh, how the angels must have struck their harps in joy once again! Finally! After several years of biting and devouring, some of those involved were willing to say those difficult words: "We were wrong."

Having agreed on these points, the Amish ministers agreed to lift the ban they had placed on the Reistians. They furthermore confessed, in writing, the errors of both sides to the Reistians and asked for Christian forbearance. To demonstrate and lead out in repentance, the Amish ministers then excommunicated themselves!

---

5   Ibid., p. 93.

Ulli Ammann later wrote about the reaction of the Reistians to this method:

> When that had happened, those on their side became very happy and, as one says, fluffed up their manes and shouted out all over saying: Now one can see who was right and who was wrong. They let themselves believe that they were excused of all mistakes and that all responsibility for the dispute was now to be found on our side alone, whereas the poor people should have been struck by the method we used on ourselves which no one else wanted to do. [This] could well have served as a warning to examine themselves and to consider what they had done to us also, and that they should also want to remove from the path the obstacles which were, after all, not insignificant and make a true path in order to be reunited. For we did not stand disciplined on account of their mistakes, but because of our own; and the mistakes which they committed have nevertheless remained.[6]

Ulli's words can possibly be read as a one-sided accusation. However, the whole spirit of Ulli in his letters is one of sadness, simply trying to state what had happened. Here, he laments that the Reistians gloated over the Amish humbling themselves, rather than joining them in humility and weeping before God.

But No Peace

After being excommunicated from the church for a time, the Amish ministers across the land approached the Reistians and asked to be reinstated. The Reistians said in writing that "regarding the matter of the quarrel, they would gladly allow and be satisfied if we would be accepted into the fellowship again, and they thought

---

6   Ibid., p. 94.

He excommunicated. . . himself?

To some, it sounds very strange to hear of a minister excommunicating himself. Note, however, that this was not only Jakob Ammann's idea—the two Palatine ministers, Hans Gut and Christian Holly, did it before he did. Moreover, several of the other Amish ministers also excommunicated themselves with Jakob Ammann. Requesting excommunication, or an ordained man excommunicating himself, is still practiced among some Old Order Amish.

Among the Swiss Brethren, for a minister to excommunicate himself may have been an accepted way for a minister to reckon with serious faults in his ministry. The *Hutterite Chronicle* records that in the 1550s, a Swiss Brethren minister excommunicated himself from the church because some of his church members—including a fellow minister—had joined the Hutterites, and the minister felt that he had failed in his duty to protect his flock.[1]

---

1 *The Chronicle of the Hutterian Brethren*, Volume I, 1987, Plough Publishing, p. 390.

we should have ourselves reinstated by them," as Ulli later wrote.[7]

The Amish agreed to be reinstated by the Reistians—but they asked two things of the Reistians: 1) confess the disputed articles of faith and 2) repent of their own rash attitudes and words. The Reistians refused and the effort for peace failed. However, the Amish ministers were reinstated into the church by ministers who had not been involved in the controversy.[8]

Many more peace meetings followed, and the two sides finally

---

7   Ibid., pp. 94-95.

8   Ibid., p. 95.

Uninvolved churches

When the Reistians refused to reinstate the Amish, some ministers who had not been involved in the controversy reinstated the Amish ministers. This reminds us of an aspect easy to overlook: Not all of the Swiss Brethren were involved in the dispute. At least some of these ministers were apparently not too prejudiced against the Amish, as they were willing to reinstate them into the church.

Sadly, in most church splits, there are a large number of people—perhaps even entire congregations—who do not feel strongly about the issues of the division and might even feel that the church would be better off not dividing. Nevertheless, they are usually forced to make a decision, because if the group divides, they cannot simply pretend that it has not.

agreed on the disputed articles, with the exception of social shunning. As it finally came to be clear, the Reistians did not agree among themselves about shunning. Ulli Ammann wrote, "In shunning, however, they were of very different minds. The one wanted more, and the other less, and the third nothing at all, namely of physical shunning."[9]

Reconciliation seemed possible, even without agreement on shunning. Some on the Reist side acknowledged the repentance and improvement of the Amish. Unfortunately, once it finally came down to this, the Reistians argued that reconciliation was still impossible because the Amish practiced footwashing, while they did not! They thus dragged out another matter, which up until that time had not been an issue. The Amish begged for peace and reconciliation, but the Reistians said that they *were* at ease on their

---

9   Ibid., p. 95.

side, and if the Amish were not, they should go back home where they came from.[10]

Even so, the Amish were not content to leave the matter there. On February 7, 1700, Amish ministers Jakob Ammann, Isaac Bachman, and Niklaus Augsburger met together to discuss again the issue of their mistakes. They together wrote a "Letter of Confession" which stated:

> We, Jakob Ammann, Isaac Bachman and Niklaus Augsburger, confess that in this controversial matter and in the harsh ban which we have used against you in Switzerland we have grievously erred. . . . We confess that the ban also applies to us, and for this reason we do not stand apart from the church without guilt, and we desire to be reconciled with God and man as much as is possible. Thus, we are asking you for forbearance, that you indeed would be willing to show us forbearance and to pray from your hearts to the Lord on our behalf that He might grant us all this through grace. For because of our error it is a matter of heartfelt concern to us that we atone for our sins while we are still living and healthy. And therefore, we are asking you once again from our hearts for forbearance, for this indeed did not happen intentionally on our part. I hope that you can believe us. Therefore, do have patience and grant us that which you are able to grant, and pray indeed to our loving God for us that He might indeed grant us all this through grace.[11]

Other Amish ministers added their own confessions and signatures to the confession, including Ulli Ammann, Christian Blank, etc. They agreed to lift the ban from the Reistians and—once again—excommunicate themselves.

---

10   Ibid.

11   Jakob Ammann et al., "Letter of Confession," in Roth, pp. 107-108.

Ironies of history

The Amish/Reistian division and its legacy through the centuries produced many ironies. Jakob Ammann had little tolerance for variation across congregations, and seems to have believed (at least in 1693, early in the dispute) that ministers should decide what to do or teach and the laity should follow. This would be a conference-type model of church administration. However, in North America, the Amish follow a more congregational model of administration, where individual congregations make decisions and relate to other congregations of like faith, but do not expect exact uniformity across all of the fellowshipping congregations. The Reist side (which came to be called Mennonites in North America) became known for creating conferences, with the ministers in each conference making decisions for the whole group which each congregation is expected to support and abide by.

The issue of names is another irony. The Amish group was espousing Dutch Mennonite views on shunning and footwashing—views which Menno Simons embraced. The Reist side was opposed to these Dutch teachings. They gave the Oberlander/Alsatian group its nickname of "Amish," which they accepted in North America, because the Reist group ended up accepting the name Mennonite when they came to North America!

Apparently following their example, Palatine minister Hans Gut produced his own "Letter of Confession." He had signed the Ohnenheim agreement with the Reistians but later (with Christian Holly, who had since died) repented and joined the Amish. He too asked the Swiss Reistians for forbearance.[12]

---

12 Hans Gut, "Letter of Confession," in Roth, p. 109.

Can you imagine a church split today in which one side would come back later and confess that they had handled the matter wrong, begging for forgiveness? Here was Jakob Ammann, the man whom the Reistians had vilified with terrible accusations, coming to them humbly, admitting his sins and errors, and begging for forgiveness—a level of humility and repentance which is amazing!

Reconciliation Refused

Unfortunately, it seems that the Reistian side did not respond to these confessions. Nevertheless, Ulli Ammann did not give up trying for peace! Nearly eleven years after this special confession by Jakob Ammann, on January 21, 1711, several Amish ministers including Ulli Ammann, Hans Anken, Jost Joder, and Hans Gut met with the Reistian ministers of Heidolsheim.[13] They asked for peace on the condition that both sides forgive each other of their errors and both would leave each other to their own views on shunning and footwashing. The Heidolsheim ministers did not say yes or no, but wrote to Switzerland for advice.[14]

It appears that in response to this plea for advice, several ministers and lay members from Switzerland and elsewhere traveled to Alsace to give a negative answer. By this time, however, the Heidolsheim ministers had already made up their minds. With rough words, they ordered the Swiss delegation out of the room and reinstated Ulli Ammann and Hans Gerber.[15]

---

13   This was the Alsatian village where Jakob and Ulli's father had died in 1695. Why Jakob was not involved in this reconciliation attempt is unknown, but he was approaching 70 years of age. It has been suggested that he was getting too old, but we simply do not know why his involvement in church relationships seems to have phased out after his plea for forgiveness. Ulli seems to have become the more prominent leader.

14   Hans Bachman et al., in Roth, pp. 111-112.

15   Christian Blank, "Summary and Defense," in Roth, pp. 118-119.

Why?

One has to ask himself a long, hard "Why?" for the rejection of this offer of reconciliation. The Amish side had done all they could do. They finally even came to the place of saying, "Let's forget all the past; you can practice social shunning (and footwashing) as you see best, and we will do as we see best." Earlier, they had wanted the Reistians to admit to wrong attitudes and that the Reistians take up social shunning. But now the Amish were willing to extend the hand of fellowship even without any admission of guilt on the Reistian side, and without demanding that the Reistians practice social shunning like the Amish did.

But some still said no. What can we conclude? While we are 300 years removed from the events, and going on limited source materials, it seems as if we can safely conclude that, in the end, the lasting division was the fault of the Reistians.

Yes, the Amish started it. Yes, the Amish—Jakob Ammann in particular—said many things they should not have said, in an un-Christ-like spirit.

But when a man confesses and asks forgiveness, even to the extent of excommunicating himself from the church until the other side is satisfied with him, what can we say?

Perhaps the best thing to say is, "Lord, have mercy on us all!"

King Louis XIV of France expelled the Anabaptists from Alsace in 1712.

CHAPTER 11

Expelled!

he Amish farmers of the Ste. Marie-aux-Mines area had done an amazing job of acquiring wealth out of the Alsatian lands devastated by war and neglect. The 1711 tax list (which included Ammann's congregation and Rudolf Hauser's congregation) gives us a glimpse of the success of the Anabaptists in the valley. Ten types of assets were considered taxable: beef cattle, chickens, goats, heifers, horses, houses, milk cows, oxen, pigs, and sheep. Between them, the two groups of Anabaptists had 260 cows, 230 goats, four chickens, and one sheep. Horses were scarce—the Anabaptists only had seven. On the other hand, they had 50 oxen.[1]

Jakob Ammann himself was not a farmer and owned only two cows, three goats, and a plot in the community garden.[2] Being a tailor, he was part of the community which earned its bread by methods other than farming. The Anabaptist community included

1   Leroy Beachy, *Unser Leit: The Story of the Amish*, 2011, Goodly Heritage Books, Volume 1, pp. 131-132.

2   Ibid.; Paul Hostettler, "The Anabaptist Amman/Ammen Families in the Alpine Foothills of Bern: Their Roots and Migration in the Period 1580 to 1713," *Pennsylvania Mennonite Heritage* 27(4) (October 2004):2-19, p. 13.

a carpenter, a knife-maker, millers, nail-makers, a shoemaker, and a tanner.

Altogether, the Amish of the Ste. Marie area owned a total value of goods equaling 12 million francs. They owned several of the best farms in the region. It has been said that the Anabaptists made up one fourth of the population and owned or leased one third of the land in the valley. This may be an overstatement, but they certainly made up a substantial percentage of the population, owned much of the land, and paid a significant amount in taxes.[3] Their wealth, however, may have proved to be their downfall.

The covetousness of government officials, who wanted the prosperous farms which had been restored by the Amish, may have been at the root of the expulsion. This cannot be proved with certainty, but there is room for suspicion.[4] Covetous officials may have pulled strings in the government to have the Anabaptists expelled.

On September 9, 1712, the provincial bailiffs of Alsace were informed of the orders of King Louis XIV. The King was a devoted Catholic who, in 1685, had taken away freedom of worship from the French Reformed (Huguenots). Now, he ordered the Alsatian government "to make leave from Alsace, with no exceptions, all the Anabaptists who established themselves there, even the oldest who had been there for a long time."[5]

The officials could not do anything about the order from the King, whether or not they wanted to carry it out. On September 10, the officials held a meeting which lasted 22 hours to discuss the mandate. They realized the severe economic consequences which

---

3   Jean Séguy, "The Bernese Anabaptists in Sainte-Marie-aux-Mines," *Pennsylvania Mennonite Heritage* 3(3) (July 1980):2-9, p. 8.

4   See Robert Baecher, "1712: Investigation of an Important Date," *Pennsylvania Mennonite Heritage* 21(2) (April 1998):2-12.

5   Ibid., p. 6.

The Anabaptist Exodus from Bern

By the early 1700s, the Bernese government was ready to resort to desperate measures to rid itself of its Anabaptists. Frustrated by Anabaptists who would be banished, promise never to return, and then return anyway, the Bernese government decided to send its Anabaptists where they could never come back! In the spring of 1710, they put 53 Anabaptists—including prominent elder Bendicht Brechtbühl—on a boat and sent them in chains down the Rhine River, bound for America against their will!

They made one miscalculation, however. The prisoners had to pass through Dutch territory. The Dutch government tolerated and valued its Mennonites, and the Mennonites had a fair amount of political clout even though they were not in government positions. Horrified by Bern's religious persecution, the Dutch government released the prisoners as soon as they set foot on Dutch soil.

The failed deportation of 1710, however, led to a new idea: Why could Bern not allow its Anabaptists to depart peaceably to a country which would accept them? The Dutch Mennonites and the Dutch government spent an immense amount of effort negotiating with the Bernese government to accomplish exactly that. In the end, the Bernese government agreed to allow the Anabaptists to sell their possessions, take the proceeds with them, and depart on five ships down the Rhine River to Holland.

The plan was a partial success. The Amish, for the most part, were willing to leave, but the Reistians—for reasons unclear—were extremely hesitant to do so, and many did not. Once on the ships, many Reistians escaped and returned to Bern at the first opportunity. On the day of departure, 307 Anabaptists showed up to leave, and 52 prisoners were put on the boats. The Amish and Reistians refused to ride together and had to be put on separate boats.

Having arrived in Holland, many of the deportees decided to stay. Eventually, some of the descendants of those Amish joined the Dutch Mennonites; others continued on to America.

would result from the implementation of the King's order. The Council sent a letter to Christian III, Palatine Count of Birkenfeld and protector of the Markirch Anabaptists. There was a concern that contracts (particularly farm leases) would be broken by the expulsion; some of the Anabaptists had contracts which would not expire until April 23. A letter was written to the King about this, and apparently the King permitted those Anabaptists to stay until their leases expired.[6]

The Anabaptists—and their sympathizers in the Alsatian government—had no choice. Prince Christian III ordered that the departing Anabaptists be given Certificates of Good Conduct.[7] The Anabaptists began to sell their properties as quickly as possible at bargain prices.[8] Some of the Anabaptists headed for the Palatinate. The Amish stayed closer, going to Lorraine, Salm, and Montbéliard. For about another century, more Amish would live in Salm (today part of France) than anywhere else in the world.

Unfortunately, some Anabaptists from the local Reistians and from Hauser's congregation decided that their farms were worth more than their faith and joined the Reformed Church, which

6   Ibid., pp. 7, 10; Leroy Beachy, *Unser Leit: The Story of the Amish*, 2011, Goodly Heritage Books, Volume 1, p. 136.

7   Robert Baecher, "1712: Investigation of an Important Date," *Pennsylvania Mennonite Heritage* 21(2) (April 1998):2-12, p. 10.

8   Ibid., p. 7.

Co-minister

Ammann's co-minister Jacob Hochstetler, known as "Preacher" Jacob Hochstetler, was probably the father of "Immigrant" Jacob Hochstetler who came to America in 1736. "Immigrant" Jacob Hochstetler (spellings for the last name vary) was the man who demonstrated nonresistance at the Northkill Amish Massacre, when some of his family members were killed and he himself taken captive by the Indians.

was still tolerated in Alsace.[9] Here we see the wisdom of Jakob Ammann's positions on the Truehearted and attendance of state church services. Some of his opponents ended up joining a church which taught that it was right to baptize babies, kill in war, swear oaths, etc.

Jakob Ammann joined those selling their possessions in order to leave Alsace. On October 25, he sold his only livestock—two cows and three goats—for 45 pounds.[10] He also sold his garden plot the same day.[11] He apparently owned no house of his own, but only leased one.

Earlier, on October 8, Jakob had "transfer[red] to Hans Farny, farmer of Monsieur de Landsberg at Zellwiller," all the money owed to him by his non-Anabaptist neighbors—a sum of 1200 pounds (approximately $60,000). He also made Hans the manager of his assets. A few months later, Jakob's co-minister Jacob

9   Ibid., p. 10.

10   Robert Baecher, "The 'Patriarche' of Sainte-Marie-aux-Mines," *Mennonite Quarterly Review* 74(1) (January 2000):145-158, p. 148.

11   Paul Hostettler, "The Anabaptist Amman/Ammen Families in the Alpine Foothills of Bern: Their Roots and Migration in the Period 1580 to 1713," *Pennsylvania Mennonite Heritage* 27(4) (October 2004):2-19, p. 13.

William Penn

Two men born in 1644 had an almost incalculable impact upon European and North American Anabaptist history. Both were raised by parents in the state churches of their respective countries. Both joined minority religious groups and became prominent leaders as adults. One was Jakob Ammann, the Amish/Anabaptist leader. The other was William Penn, the Quaker.

Born in 1644 and dying in 1718, William Penn's life matched Jakob Ammann's almost exactly, although they never crossed paths personally, as far as we know. Penn was the son of an admiral in the British Navy, who wanted his son to live the life of an aristocratic English gentleman. He was sorely disappointed by his son's decision to join the Quakers, a despised and persecuted religious group which emphasized the importance of the "Light of Christ Within" and refused to go to war or swear oaths.

Young William Penn became a prominent Quaker leader, traveling and preaching for the movement, interceding with the government for religious toleration, and writing defenses of Quaker teachings. He suffered imprisonment for his faith more than once himself.

In 1681, in repayment of a debt which the government owed William's deceased father, King Charles II granted William a charter for a colony in America, called Pennsylvania or "Penn's Woods." (William insisted that the name referred to his father and not himself.) William Penn envisioned a colony with freedom of religion for all, and sought settlers from persecuted minorities in Europe. Anglicans (members of the English state church), however, were also welcome. Penn also tried to treat the Native Americans fairly, paying them for land which the king had "given" him, although whether

the Indians always saw him as fair is another question. Pennsylvania also permitted slavery at first, and Penn himself owned some slaves, whom he freed in his will.

The first permanent Mennonite settlement in North America was in Germantown, where some Dutch Mennonites settled in 1683. The congregation was not formally organized until some time later. Eventually, thousands of Mennonites and Amish would pour into eastern Pennsylvania, and from there would spread across the continent. They left Europe, which refused (with some exceptions) to tolerate them, to America, where they could build lives, farms, and churches in freedom.

Pennsylvania was in some ways a political and economic disaster for William. He never received the economic rewards he expected from the colony, and political tensions and controversies demanded his strength and attention for most of his life. However, while Pennsylvania was not the first colony in America to offer religious freedom, it did demonstrate that people of different religions could live together harmoniously, although it also demonstrated that when nonresistant people such as Quakers tried to rule the government, the results were very disappointing.

Hochstetler declared that "Jacquy Aman" had been paid in full.[12, 13]

What happened to Jakob after this? He may have gone to live with or near Hans Farny.[14] However, we do not know for sure. Jakob's last days remain shrouded in mystery. He did not receive a Certificate of Good Conduct, as far as we know.[15]

We have one clue in the form of an entry in the *Journal of the Anabaptist Chamber* of Bern. On Wednesday, April 12, 1730, an entry was recorded regarding "a daughter of the late Anabaptist minister Jacob Ammen from Erlenbach, who died outside the country." From this we learn that Jakob died before April 1730, somewhere outside of Bern. Unfortunately, the report does not give Jakob's daughter's name. The full entry reads as follows:

Wednesday, the 12th April, 1730. Wimmis. Because the presenter of this, which she alleges, is a daughter of the late Anabaptist minister Jacob Ammen from Erlenbach, who died outside the country, requests to receive the Holy baptism, and to be taken up in the bosom of the church. So the official of the chamber of Anabaptists will kindly implore Mr. Castlahnen to make the proper arrangements, that this person could be instructed and prepared by the Honorable preachers at Erlenbach. When this has been done by them, then this person shall be publicly baptized in this church house. Which, then, when she has been baptized, shall pay 4 dollars for the ceremony and the official. Wimmis.

[Separate entry] Erlenbach, to the Honorable Preachers, officials of

12   Robert Baecher, "The 'Patriarche' of Sainte-Marie-aux-Mines," *Mennonite Quarterly Review* 74(1) (January 2000):145-158, p. 148.

13   Paul Hostettler, "The Anabaptist Amman/Ammen Families in the Alpine Foothills of Bern: Their Roots and Migration in the Period 1580 to 1713," *Pennsylvania Mennonite Heritage* 27(4) (October 2004):2-19, p. 13.

14   Robert Baecher, "The 'Patriarche' of Sainte-Marie-aux-Mines," *Mennonite Quarterly Review* 74(1) (January 2000):145-158, p. 148.

15   Ibid., p. 156.

Could Jakob Ammann read?

[signature: Jacob Amm...]

This is Jakob Ammann's signature on an Alsatian government document. It looks like the signature of someone who has no problem reading and writing. But wait—there is a problem. It is not Jakob's at all! Someone else had signed for him!

[mark: i.AMME]

Jakob Ammann's real signature looks like this. Most often, he simply signed his initials, "iA." Ammann signed his initials to 37 known documents, and his initials are often followed by the note, "Jacob Ammann, not being able to write, has only made his mark."

[mark: iA]

The fact that Ammann could not write, and signed his name in a crude, blocky script, naturally raises the question of whether he could read. Further questions are raised by the account of Ammann's meeting with Rudolph Hauser and Peter Lehman, where Ammann asked one of them to read a letter (see page 135). However, since this was a meeting between several men, it could have just been natural for one person to read aloud a letter which they were going to discuss.

Just because Jakob Ammann could not write does not mean he could not read; however, we have no solid proof that he could read. His "Long Letter" is the product of a person with significant Bible knowledge, but he could have gained that through people reading to him. However, as a businessman with at least some level of economic success, it is easy to assume he would have needed at least basic literacy.

We simply do not know whether he could read or not. The art on this book's cover portrays Jakob eagerly drinking in the words of Scripture. Was he able to drink in the words of life through reading?

the Chamber of Anabaptists. Let the same, by this, be kindly implored, by the presenter of this, the daughter of the late Anabaptist Minister, Jacob Amman, who died outside of the country, who desires to receive Holy baptism, and to be taken up in the bosom of our church. Also to be instructed in our religion, to be prepared for this Holy undertaking. When then this person, according to the honorable Pastor's understanding, has been sufficiently prepared and instructed, she shall be baptized publicly in front of the congregation in the church, after which Mr. Castlahnen, when she has been baptized, shall be given some payment for performing the ceremony. Wimmis.[16]

We do not know why Jakob's daughter attempted to join the Reformed Church; there is no evidence that she ever actually did join them. No record of her baptism has been found, and no record of the payment has been discovered.[17] It has been speculated that she wanted Bernese citizenship, but when she found that it would be necessary to receive Reformed baptism, she gave up that idea.

The expulsion of 1712 was only partially successful in eliminating

---

16   John Hüppi, "Identifying Jacob Ammann," *Mennonite Quarterly Review* 74(2) (April 2000):329-339, p. 331; translated by Josiah Beachy. Wimmis is on the south shore of Lake Thun in Canton Bern.

17   John Hüppi, "Identifying Jacob Ammann," *Mennonite Quarterly Review* 74(2) (April 2000):329-339, pp. 331-332.

the Anabaptists from Alsace. Many Anabaptists stayed on "under-ground." In fact, it is possible that some of Jakob's own relatives were able to stay. Amish bishop Ulrich Sommer was married to a woman by the name of Barbara Ammin, who was quite possi-bly Jakob's granddaughter or possibly related in some other way. Her death record says: "Barbara Ammin, wife of Ulrich Sommers, bookbinder in Landhaus, died in childbirth on July 2, 1743 at the age of 33."[18]

What about Ulrich Ammann? About 1720, he wrote a letter to the congregation in Markirch giving advice about how to handle problems and disagreements. It contains the wisdom of a church leader who had known the bitter price of failure in maintaining peace in church relationships.[19] He was still living in Canton Neuchatel as of 1733.[20]

Thus the Ammann brothers fade off the scene of history. Their lives left a legacy which continues to this day, in the hundreds of thousands of Amish and Amish-Mennonites living in North America and elsewhere. They left a legacy of uncompromising obedience to the teachings of Scripture, but also one which was stained by impatience. They left a legacy of humility and peace in their effort to bring reconciliation between the two Swiss Brethren factions, but their failure in this effort reminds us that sometimes, not even the most sincere repentance can undo the harm done by our sin.

By the time of Jakob Ammann's death, a new chapter in Anabaptist history had begun. Swiss Brethren were crossing the

18   Robert Baecher, "The 'Patriarche' of Sainte-Marie-aux-Mines," *Mennonite Quarterly Review* 74(1) (January 2000):145-158, p. 154.

19   Ulli Ammann, "Ulli Ammann to the Congregation at Markirch," in Roth, pp. 121-125. See appendix.

20   Hanspeter Jecker, personal correspondence.

Atlantic to participate in William Penn's "Holy Experiment" in Pennsylvania. They went to build new lives in America, free of the problems and persecutions of Europe. The sea shunned no one.[21]

---

21   Steven M. Nolt, *A History of the Amish*, 2003, Good Books, p. 50.

Ulrich Ammann's Letter to the Church in Markirch (c. 1720)

In this letter, seemingly written c. 1720, Ulli Ammann gives advice to the congregation at Markirch about how issues are to be decided in the church and how the ministry and laity are to live together in peace and harmony. The letter's loving tone, as well as some of its specific recommendations, indicate that Ammann was writing out of bitter experience and regret for the mistakes of the past. He recommends a peaceful working together between the congregation and its ministry, with the congregation respecting its ordained men's directions, while the ministry are not to think they always have to have the last word. He also says that minor differences between congregations are not cause for concern, and traditional practices—as long as they are not in conflict with God's Word—are best left as they are, and effort given rather to "break[ing] down the old, carnal, sinful life of humans" and "implant[ing] a new godly life."

This translation is from John D. Roth, *Letters of the Amish Division*, 2nd edition, 2002, Mennonite Historical Society, pp. 121-125. Used by permission.

A copy of a letter which Ulli Ammann sent to the ministers and elders of the congregation at Markirch.

A sincere brotherly greeting, with the wish for the very best for your soul and body in time and eternity, to all the beloved fellow ministers who have helped with the work in the house of the Lord, also to the brothers and sisters who by God's grace are partakers with us in the same faith and worship. Think well of us in your prayers of which we are in great need.

For the sake of peace and unity, and to ward off quarrels as much as possible, it has seemed good to us to make known by means of the following letter what our understanding and opinion is in these following points: namely, that a minister and overseer of a congregation—at whatever place he may be, an ordained man or a fully confirmed man who is called an elder—can save himself from guilt and the accusations of others in no better way than to proceed with counsel in those matters of consequence that occur in the congregation. We think it is also his duty to do this when something controversial or other important matters arise in the congregation, that he should first of all take counsel with his fellow ministers and then also with the congregation.

It is our understanding that an elder or ordained minister does indeed have authority to make his presentation first about the things which happened and may suggest a model of what he thinks to be best, and then he may present it to his fellow ministers and to the congregation to consider and turn it over to them to correct as much as they can from the Word of God. He should not think that his presentation must be the only valid one and that no one should have anything to say against it, or that even though ten or twenty brethren oppose it, the minister's word must be king, as Hans Anken in Holland said.

But if no one has a valid—we repeat, a valid—objection (and

not something based on spite or ill-will, as can easily happen) to the minister's or elder's initial presentation, then it should be confirmed by the consent of the congregation. But if it should happen, as it easily could, that the general counsel does not turn out for the best, then the minister who made the initial presentation does not bear the sole responsibility; the entire congregation helps to bear the blame with him and the congregation then has no authority or right to put the blame entirely on him.

If it should happen that the minister's or elder's initial presentation on some important matter was not generally understood to be the best and dissension then followed, and some supported the elder and his initial presentation while the opposing party thought they could not support it, then we think they should not argue about it to the point where love is lost. Nor should the minister think that the opposing party must bend to his understanding and that he would gladly like to rule over them contrary to their conscience, as Hans Anken did in Holland which resulted in such great harm.

The elder and those who support his initial presentation, and the opposing party which feels that they cannot accept it, should come to an agreement and let the matter come to other elders and ministers in other congregations to examine and to discuss according to their best understanding, and then both sides should be content to adapt themselves to it as far as is possible so that it might promote the general peace from the elder's side as well as on the other side.

Oh, if only this could happen, which would be very necessary and good, that all elders and ministers would follow Christ's example in all that is good, and especially in humble and scriptural obedience to God, and could give the people a good model, and that a domineering nature which is very closely related to destructive

pride would be given no place. As Peter says: Not as those who
rule over the inheritance, rather become an example to the flock
(1 Peter 5). Also, if someone has made you a ruler, do not put on
airs; but rather be as one among the people, says Sirach 32. Also,
the appointed king of Israel should not lift his heart up above his
brethren. Also, the Savior said: You know that the worldly princes
rule over the peoples, and the overlords act with authority. But it
should not be so among you. Just as the Son of Man did not come
to be served, but to serve and to give his life as a ransom for the
multitude (Matthew 20). From these words one cannot draw the
meaning that freedom is granted a minister in the Lord's church to
dominate but, on the other hand, neither should it be understood to
mean that one has the freedom to treat an elder or minister poorly
and unkindly, as can easily happen at times.

We are obligated and duty-bound to give help and support to
faithful ministers and leaders of the church of the Lord, for they
are a gift of God, and not allow them to be trampled on unjustly,
accepting no complaint against them except from the mouths of
two or three witnesses (I Timothy 5). We should love and respect
them and give them appropriate honor and service, as the Apostle
Paul admonishes in this regard: the elders who lead well are worthy
of double honor and reward, especially those who labor in the Word
and in teaching (I Timothy 5). Also, we ask you, dear brothers,
that you recognize those who labor among you, and who lead you
in the Lord and who admonish you, that you hold them in even
greater love because of their work, and are at peace with them
(I Thessalonians 5). Also, submit yourselves to them that rule over
you, for they watch over your souls as ones who must give account
for them (Hebrews 13). But one who puffs himself up and speaks
more out of hostility than with justification against a faithful minister of the Lord and leader of His congregation who speaks and

acts in an exemplary manner, and thinks that one may surely speak against [the minister] and not simply accept everything he says as valid—Korah with his mob indeed found out what kind of pleasure the Lord takes in such wrongful rebels and gainsayers (Numbers 16). Because disobedient Israel did not love the good prophets sent by God but contradicted them and hated and persecuted them unto death, God therefore punished Israel and allowed false prophets to come in great numbers.

Holy Scripture provides plenty of instruction on how leaders and followers are to conduct themselves toward each other. The Apostle says: The younger are subject to the older, and all are subject to one another in the fear of God thereby showing humility (I Peter 5). We also consider it necessary and good that a minister strive to keep order by maintaining the old, traditional practices of the church, not doing much that is new and out of the ordinary, or breaking with the old. It is better that he continue with the teachings of the divine Word and to break down the old, carnal, sinful life of humans and to implant a new godly life.

If, however, something that is useless and contrary to the Word of the Lord would be the practice in the congregation, it must of necessity be dropped and in its place a better practice should be established in harmony with the Lord's Word. This we think should indeed be done, but no one should undertake to do it by himself without the knowledge and counsel of other ministers and elders. Tobit says: Always ask counsel of the wise (Tobit 4). Do nothing without counsel, and after the deed you will not regret it (Sirach 32).

It is, of course, possible that one congregation has a practice not found in another, but only unimportant and minor things which are not in conflict with the Word of the Lord. Against such things one should not complain, but rather plead the cause of love and peace.

This is a small portion, presented in simplicity and brevity, of what we think is necessary and good for a minister and also for the congregation and which serves the cause of peace, for in peace God has called us through Jesus Christ, Amen. Whoever also accepts this as good, and wants to help work to this end, may sign below if they so desire.

Date 1703[1]

Ulli Ammann

---

1   Although the manuscript copy is dated 1703, Ammann's references in the letter to Hans Anken of Holland suggest a more likely date of 1720.—*Trans.*

But if you love the neighbor, you will not scold or ban zealously, will not seek your own, will not remember evil, will not be ambitious or puffed up, but kind, righteous, generous in all gifts, humble and sympathetic with the weak and imperfect.[1]

—Michael Sattler

1   Michael Sattler, Letter to the Church at Horb, 1527; translation from *The Legacy of Michael Sattler*, trans. and ed. by John H. Yoder, p. 59. © Herald Press. Used with permission. All rights reserved.

APPENDIX B

Reflections on Shunning

We also believe in, and confess, a ban, Separation, and Christian correction in the church, for amendment, and not for destruction, in order to distinguish that which is pure from the impure: namely, when any one, after he is enlightened, has accepted the knowledge of the truth, and been incorporated into the communion of the saints, sins again unto death, either through willfulness, or through presumption against God, or through some other cause, and falls into the unfruitful works of darkness, thereby becoming separated from God, and forfeiting the kingdom of God, that such a one... may not remain in the congregation of the righteous, but, as an offensive member and open sinner, shall and must be separated, put away, reproved before all, and purged out as leaven...that the sinner may not be condemned with the world, but become convinced in his mind, and be moved to sorrow, repentance, and reformation... Concerning the withdrawing from, or shunning the separated, we believe and confess, that if any one, either through his wicked life or perverted doctrine, has so far fallen that he is separated from God, and, consequently, also separated and punished by the church, the same must, according to the doctrine of Christ and His apostles,

be shunned, without distinction, by all the fellow members of the
church, especially those to whom it is known, in eating, drinking,
and other similar intercourse, and no company be had with him…
Yet, in shunning as well as in reproving, such moderation and
Christian discretion must be used, that it may conduce, not to the
destruction, but to the reformation of the sinner. For, if he is needy,
hungry, thirsty, naked, sick, or in any other distress, we are in duty
bound, necessity requiring it, according to love and the doctrine of
Christ and His apostles, to render him aid and assistance; otherwise, shunning would in this case tend more to destruction than
to reformation.

—Dortrecht Confession, Articles 16 & 17

Martyrs Mirror, p. 43

While all the scriptural Anabaptists believed that open sinners should be excommunicated from the congregation until they
repent, the Dutch Mennonites took the view—championed by
Menno Simons—that Paul's words in I Corinthians 5:11 mean
that church members cannot eat social meals with those who had
been excommunicated. Jakob Ammann, and the Amish to this
day, agree.

Unfortunately, some Anabaptist groups today have taken the
concept of "shunning"—and of church discipline in general—and
have exaggerated it to monstrous extremes. The authors of this
book do not support unchristian and extreme shunning and discipline, attempts to manipulate and coerce people with threats of
excommunication, or the use of excommunication and/or shunning
as weapons in church disputes. Any use of excommunication and/
or shunning which transgresses and violates the Spirit of Christ is
not Christian. It is easy for excommunication to become a carnal
weapon wielded in a carnal way.

This does not mean that church discipline, excommunication, and withdrawing from unrepentant sinners are unscriptural. They are, and must be used in the Spirit of Christ for the restoration of sinners and the preservation of the church. (See Matthew 18:15-18, I Corinthians 5, II Thessalonians 3:6-15, I Timothy 1:20, and Titus 3:10-11.) Furthermore, it needs to be said that what some groups in North America practice is itself an exaggeration or a caricature of what Menno Simons and Jakob Ammann themselves taught. Keep in mind that excommunication is to be done out of love, for the restoration of the sinner. With typical ardent zeal, Menno wrote:

> If you see your brother sin, then do not pass him by as one that does not value his soul; but if his fall be curable, from that moment endeavor to raise him up by gentle admonition and brotherly instruction, before you eat, drink, sleep, or do anything else, as one who ardently desires his salvation, lest your poor erring brother harden and be ruined in his fall, and perish in his sin. . . . But if such things [true repentance] are found in them, in good faith, as before God who sees all things, then we say, Welcome, beloved brethren! Welcome, beloved sisters! And we rejoice beyond measure at the sincere conversion of such brethren and sisters as one rejoices at the restoration of an only son who is healed of a critical and deadly disease, or a lost sheep or penny that is found again, or at the appearance of a son who was given up as lost.[1]

We must keep the church pure by using excommunication when a sinner in the midst of the church refuses to repent. We must keep the unleavened loaf safe from leaven by avoiding those who are

---

1 Menno Simons, *Admonition on Church Discipline*, 1541, in J. C. Wenger, *The Complete Writings of Menno Simons*, Herald Press, pp. 411-414. © Herald Press. Used with permission. All rights reserved.

hardened in sin and wish to turn us away from obedience to Christ. While harsh and un-Christ-like shunning is wrong, there is also a danger in continuing to have social fellowship with an excommunicated and unrepentant sinner. As Paul says, the leaven could spread. There are spiritual casualties which warn of the danger of holding fellowship with the unrighteous.

We must not allow this reality to drive us to extremes, to unchristian and harsh banning and shunning, and when we do have a member who has been excommunicated, we must do as God (and Menno Simons) instruct, praying and laboring for his restoration.

MQR = *Mennonite Quarterly Review*

PMH = *Pennsylvania Mennonite Heritage*

The Chronicle of the Hutterian Brethren. Volume I. 1987. Plough Publishing.

"Heritage." http://www.saintemarieauxmines.fr/la-ville/patri-moine (Accessed June 30, 2020).

Baecher, Robert. "1712: Investigation of an Important Date." *PMH* 21(2) (April 1998):2-12.

Baecher, Robert. "The 'Patriarche' of Sainte-Marie-aux-Mines." *MQR* 74(1) (January 2000):145-158.

Baecher, Robert. "From Steffisburg to Ste. Marie-aux-Mines: The Exodus of Those Who Would Become Amish, Part I." *Mennonite Family History* 23(1) (January 2004):4-16.

Baecher, Robert. "From Steffisburg to Ste. Marie-aux-Mines: The Exodus of Those Who Would Become Amish, Part II." *Mennonite Family History* 23(2) (April 2004):69-81.

Beachy, Leroy. *Unser Leit: The Story of the Amish*. 2011. Goodly Heritage Books.

Furner, Mark. 1998. "The Repression and Survival of Anabaptism in the Emmental, Switzerland 1659-1743: A Dissertation." Dissertation. University of Cambridge.

Furner, Mark. "On the Trail of Jacob Ammann." *MQR* 74(2) (April 2000):326-328.

Gratz, Delbert L. "The Home of Jakob Amman in Switzerland." *MQR* 25(2) (April 1951):137-139.

Gratz, Delbert L. *Bernese Anabaptists and Their American Descendants*. 1953. Mennonite Historical Society.

Gross, Leonard. Editor. *Golden Apples in Silver Bowls.* 1999. Lancaster Mennonite Historical Society.

Hege, Lydie, & Christoph Wiebe. Editors. *The Amish: Origin and Characteristics 1693-1993.* 1996. Association Française d'Histoire Anabaptiste-Mennonite.

Hostetler, John A. *Amish Society.* 4th edition. 1993. Johns Hopkins University Press.

Hostettler, Paul. "The Anabaptist Amman/Ammen Families in the Alpine Foothills of Bern: Their Roots and Migration in the Period 1580 to 1713." *PMH* 27(4) (October 2004):2-19.

Hüppi, John. "Identifying Jacob Ammann." *MQR* 74(2) (April 2000):329-339.

Jecker, Hanspeter. "Jakob Ammanns missglückte Verhaftung im Bernbiet 1694." *Mennonitica Helvetica* 18 (1995).

Jecker, Hanspeter (with Heinrich Löffler). "'Wie dem schädlichen Übel der Taüfferey zu remedieren sey' - Zwei Briefe des Pfarrers Johann Rudolf Salchli von Eggiwil im Emmental (1693f.)." *Mennonitica Helvetica* 28/29 (2005/2006):89-145.

Jecker, Hanspeter. "The Emergence of the Amish (1693ff.): Chronology and Background to the Collapse of an Ecclesial Transformation Process." *MQR* 94(4) (October 2020):539-556.

Keller, Hans Gustav. "Aus dem Leben eines bernischen Landvogts: Karl Manuel, Schultheiss in Thun 1686-1692." *Neues Berner Taschenbuch B.* 37, 1931.

Leu, Urs B., & Christian Scheidegger. Editors. *Die Zürcher Täufer 1525-1700.* 2007. Theologischer Verlag Zurich.

Lowry, James. Translator and editor. *Hans Landis.* 2003. Ohio Amish Library.

Lowry, James. Translator and editor. *Documents of Brotherly Love, Volume I.* 2007. Ohio Amish Library.

Lowry, James. Translator and editor. *Documents of Brotherly Love, Volume II.* 2015. Ohio Amish Library.

McGrath, William R. Editor. *Christlicher Ordnung or Christian Discipline.* 1966. Pathway Publishing.

Müller, Ernst. *History of the Bernese Anabaptists.* 1895. Translation by John A. Gingerich. 2010. Pathway Publishers.

Nolt, Steven M. *A History of the Amish.* 2003. Good Books.

Oyer, John S. *They Harry the Good People Out of the Land.* 2000. Mennonite Historical Society.

Roth, John D. *Letters of the Amish Division: A Sourcebook.* 2nd edition. 2002. Mennonite Historical Society.

Séguy, Jean. "The Bernese Anabaptists in Sainte-Marie-aux-Mines." *PMH* 3(3) (July 1980):2-9.

Springer, Joe A. "'The Anabaptist Amman/Ammen Families': A Response." *PMH* 28(1) (January 2005):24-25.

Staker, Joseph Peter. *Amish Mennonites in Tazewell County, Illinois.* 2017. Self-published. www.tcghs.org/links.htm.

Thormann, George. *Probier-Stein.* 1693. Translated by Katharina Epp. 2005.

Wenger, J. C. Editor. *The Complete Writings of Menno Simons.* 1984. Herald Press.

Zürcher, Isaac. "Hans Reist House and the 'Vale of Anabaptists.'" *MQR* 66(3) (July 1992):426-427.

Sidebar sources

Burkholder, Dale. *The Scriptures: Preserved and Translated.* Forthcoming. Grace Press.

Marteilhe, Jean. *Galley Slave.* 2010 (reprint). Seaforth Publishing.

Murphy, Andrew R. *William Penn: A Life.* 2019. Oxford University Press.

Shantz, Douglas H. *An Introduction to German Pietism*. 2013. Johns Hopkins University Press.

Vincent, John Martin. "European Blue Laws." *Annual Report of the American Historical Association* (1897):355-372.

Vincent, John Martin. *Costume and Conduct in the Laws of Basel, Bern, and Zurich 1370-1800*. 1935. Johns Hopkins University Press.

Cover—Ammann family. By Peter Balholm. Copyright © 2020 Sermon on the Mount Publishing.

Title page—Jakob Ammann's signature from an Alsatian government document. Provided by Robert Baecher.

p. 3—Erlenbach Reformed chapel. © Wikipedia user: Schleppyca. CC A-S A 3.0 Unported (https://creativecommons.org/licenses/by-sa/3.0/legalcode).

p. 6—SARS-CoV-2 (novel coronavirus). © National Institute of Allergy and Infectious Diseases. CC A 2.0 Generic (https://creativecommons.org/licenses/by/2.0/legalcode). *Yersinia pestis*. National Institutes of Health. Public domain.

p. 7—Battle of Rocroi. © Augusto Ferrer-Dalmau. CC A-S A 3.0 (https://creativecommons.org/licenses/by-sa/3.0/legalcode).

p. 9—Map. © Lancaster Mennonite Historical Society; used by permission.

p. 13—Weapons. Public domain. Nikolaus Leuenberger. Public domain.

p. 16—Simmental Valley. © Wikipedia user: Hadi. CC A 2.5 Generic (http://creativecommons.org/licenses/by/2.5/legalcode).

p. 19—Interior of Erlenbach chapel. © Wikipedia user WillYs Fotowerkstatt. CC A 3.0 Unported (http://creativecommons.org/licenses/by/3.0/legalcode).

p. 23—Possible Ammann family home. Provided by © Thomas Kaltenreider. CC A-S A 3.0 Unported (http://creativecommons.org/licenses/by-sa/3.0/legalcode).

p. 24—Oberhofen am Thunersee. © Dietrich Michael Weidmann. CC A-S A 3.0 Unported (http://creativecommons.org/licenses/by-sa/3.0/legalcode).

p. 25—Map. © Lancaster Mennonite Historical Society; used by permission.

p. 32—Castle of Thun. © Ruedi Fahrni. CC A-S A 3.0 Unported (http://creativecommons.org/licenses/by-sa/3.0/legalcode).

p. 34—*Chorgerichtsmanual* entry. Provided by Hanspeter Jecker.

pp. 40-41—Timeline. Prepared by Clement Ebersole. © Sermon on the Mount Publishing.

p. 42—Catharina Müller. *Martyrs Mirror* illustration by Jan Luyken. Public domain.

pp. 64-65—Map. From James Lowry, translator and editor, *Documents of Brotherly Love*, Volume II, 2015, Ohio Amish Library, p. 474. Used by permission.

p. 110—Steffisburg. Public domain.

p. 113—Galley ship. Public domain.

p. 115—Ste. Marie-aux-Mines. © Bernard Chenal. CC A SA 3.0 Unported (https://creativecommons.org/licenses/by-sa/3.0/legalcode).

p. 116—Jakob Ammann house. © Dean Taylor; used by permission.

p. 118—Ste. Marie valley. © Dean Taylor; used by permission.

p. 121—Jakob Ammann house. © David Bercot; used by permission.

p. 126—Swiss Anabaptist man. Mathias Gabriel Lory (1784-1846), c. 1825. Courtesy Mennonite Historical Library, Goshen, Indiana.

p. 127—Swiss Anabaptist woman. Mathias Gabriel Lory (1784-1846), c. 1825. Courtesy Mennonite Historical Library, Goshen, Indiana.

p. 131—Rue Jacob Amann road sign. © David Bercot; used by permission.

p. 146—King Louis XIV. Public domain.

p. 153—William Penn. Public domain.

p. 155—Ammann signatures. Provided by Robert Baecher.